DECOLONIZING the BODY

Healing,
Body-Centered
Practices for
Women of Color
to Reclaim
Confidence,
Dignity &
Self-Worth

Kelsey Blackwell

New Harbinger Publications, Inc.

Publisher's Note

NEW HARBINGER PUBLICATIONS is a registered trademark of New Harbinger Publications, Inc.

New Harbinger Publications is an employee-owned company.

Cover design by Sara Christian

Acquired by Jennye Garibaldi

Edited by Gretel Hakanson

Library of Congress Cataloging-in-Publication Data

Names: Blackwell, Kelsey, author.
Title: Decolonizing the body : healing, body-centered practices for women of color
   to reclaim confidence, dignity, and self-worth / Kelsey Blackwell.
Description: Oakland, CA : New Harbinger Publications, [2023] | Includes
   bibliographical references.
Identifiers: LCCN 2022045189 | ISBN 9781648480614 (trade paperback)
Subjects: LCSH: Mind and body. | Self-actualization (Psychology) | Mind and body
   therapies. | Minority women--Psychology. | Colonization. | BISAC: SELF-HELP
   / Personal Growth / General | FAMILY & RELATIONSHIPS / Prejudice
Classification: LCC BF151 .B53 2023 | DDC 158.1--dc23/eng/20221122
LC record available at https://lccn.loc.gov/2022045189

Printed in the United States of America

25   24   23

10   9   8   7   6   5   4   3   2   1   First Printing

"*Decolonizing the Body* is a vital offering to women of color seeking a somatic approach to community healing. Practical, earthy, and wise, Blackwell invites us to do the inner work, and is a trustworthy guide for our time."

—**Ruth King**, author of *Mindful of Race: Transforming Racism from the Inside Out*

"*Decolonizing the Body* is beautifully written, instructive, and inspiring. In accessible but flowing language, Kelsey Blackwell starts by reminding us that the body never lies. She helps us remember how to hear its signals, and even more importantly, provides a practical guide to freeing ourselves from the boxes that patriarchy, racism, and capitalism try to force us into."

—**Rinku Sen**, social justice strategist, and author of *Stir It Up*

"This book is filled with so many moments of wisdom and joy. It is a gentle beckoning to one's sensing, one's feeling, one's freedom. Naming the lies of internalized colonization and the truths of interdependence, unconditional dignity, and more, Kelsey weaves an invitation. Importantly, this book is written by and for women of color. And those of us who are white have so much to gain from reading it, too."

—**Staci K. Haines**, author of *The Politics of Trauma*, and cofounder of generative somatics and generationFIVE

"*Decolonizing the Body* feels like a delicious exhale—an irresistible unclenching that paves way for the heart's gentle opening, making our collective healing and liberation possible from within."

—**Michelle MiJung Kim**, award-winning author of *The Wake Up*, and CEO and cofounder of Awaken

"If *Decolonizing the Body* strives toward understanding the complexities of individualism and interdependence, I believe there is an independence that comes with humanity. In indigenous belief systems, community brings harmony. So, our gifts come with a deeper understanding of ourselves as individuals, divinely endowed, calling us to interwoven harmony and interdependence with all living organisms birthed on Mother Earth."

—**Therese Taylor-Stinson**, author of *Walking the Way of Harriet Tubman*

"Through simply relatable stories, clear guidance for remembrance, and kind invitations, Kelsey weaves an embodied way forward—amidst and beyond our systematic programming—into the love and wisdom that already lives within us."

—**Chetna Mehta**, artist, facilitator, and founder of Mosaiceye

"Kelsey Blackwell's beautiful book invites us to attend with kindness to our individual and social bodies as a pathway to insight, healing, and confidence. She reflects on the imprints of racism that live in our bodies, and she offers journaling and body-based mindfulness practices that support our transformation toward freedom in this world of suffering and injustice. Her buoyant style inspires us to not give up, but to discover true joy in the challenge."

> —**Arawana Hayashi**, cocreator of Social Presencing Theater with
> the Presencing Institute, and author of *Social Presencing Theater*

"In *Decolonizing the Body*, Kelsey provides a deeply needed antidote, balm, and guide to BIPOC women seeking an embodied path away from the imprints of dominance and internalized forces of oppression. Her very words—clear, planted, compassionate, and wise—serve as an ancestral gift, a lantern that rekindles our own within, helping to reset our nervous systems and restore us to our birthrights. This book is a sacred text."

> —**Colleen (Coke) Tani, MSW, MFA, MDiv**, spiritual director,
> writer, dancer, certified InterPlay leader, and teaching mentor

"Kelsey's critical, political, and inviting approach to decolonization and embodiment is a key to self-acceptance in a world that teaches us to reject who we inherently are. Participating in Kelsey's Decolonizing the Body course shifted my own practices, and this book is a careful, nuanced summary of wisdom that has the power to change the way we approach both individual and collective healing."

> —**Jezz Chung**, multidisciplinary artist; and author of
> the upcoming book, *This Way to Change*

"Reading Kelsey Blackwell's book, *Decolonizing the Body*, with tears of joy in my heart for all the people who will take their own healing journey because of her gifts—for words, for somatic healing, for honoring our ancestors. We are being given an opportunity to remember, reclaim, release, and relate to ourselves and one another with embodied authenticity and unparalleled freedom. Thank you for your heart, your withness, and your example, Kelsey."

> —**Kira Lynne Allen**, certified InterPlay leader,
> and author of *Write This Second*

For my sisters, Daryl and Carlynn.

And for all my sisters.

Contents

Foreword

I often wonder how my ancestor Harriet Tubman had the audacity to believe that she was worthy of freedom. In my daydreams, I like to imagine Harriet awakening one seemingly ordinary day, getting dressed, anointing her radiant ebony skin with shea butter, and brushing her glorious 4C black hair. Then, while exiting her plantation cabin and surveying the glistening sun rising above the milky cotton fields, Harriet simply shakes her head and says to herself, "I'm too sacred for this."

Born into slavery in 1822 and socially and religiously programmed to remain dutifully enslaved her entire life, no one knows exactly *how* Harriet deprogrammed herself in a wicked colonial system designed to tether and diminish her. Indeed, the mere physical and emotional brutality of slavery practically forced my ancestors to disconnect from their bodies, emotions, and desires, thus making it nearly impossible for them to connect with their deep embodied wisdom. As Kelsey Blackwell writes in this wonderful book, "our people...learned to push our anger far down, to disconnect from feeling and sensation 'to get through,' to feel shame for ourselves and our bodies."

Despite this forceful colonial programming, Harriet somehow resisted, tapped into her deep embodied wisdom, faced her terror, relinquished her colonial attachments, charted a liberation path, and then returned to help set others free. Wow.

I have often wished for access to Harriet's freedom map. For I, too, have longed for liberation from our society's colonial entrapments. I have longed to know *how* Harriet resisted, *how* she connected to her deep embodied wisdom, *how* she faced her terror, *how* she relinquished her colonial attachments, and *how* she charted a liberation path. If you too are longing for the *how* of the freedom journey, then *Decolonizing the Body* is for you. For within this gift of a book, Kelsey Blackwell wisely, compassion-ately, and fiercely shows us *how* to connect with our deep body wisdom so we can get free like Mama Harriet. Indeed, my *head* knows this book is full of invaluable wisdom because I have been lucky enough to read an early version. But even more importantly, my *body* knows this book is full of invaluable wisdom because I have been a student of Kelsey's for three years—and, as a result, my body is freer than ever.

I met Kelsey just two months after I quit my job as a professor at Duke University, a plantation-like work environment with a towering campus chapel that boasted a life-size statue of Robert E. Lee among the Judeo-Christian saints. I, like Harriet Tubman, had awakened to the reality that I was simply too sacred to remain enslaved any longer. Now, I was finally ready to prioritize my embodied wisdom over the head knowledge I had acquired through my many years in academia. There was just one problem: I didn't know how to connect with my body, much less its wisdom. For as I would come to learn through the teachings of Kelsey, getting off the plan-tation is as much an internal process as it is an external process.

Though I had escaped the Duke plantation, many internal plantations remained within me and were evident among my seemingly insurmount-able disconnect from my body, my suppressed and indecipherable emotions, my obsession with perfection and so-called "efficiency," and the absolute terror that arose within my skin when I considered the mere possibility of taking time to genuinely rest in the midst of our capitalistic society. I may have physically escaped the plantation, but I was still very much enslaved to fear. Indeed, when I first encountered Kelsey at an in-person, BIPOC body wisdom class, just taking a deep breath at her invitation felt stressful because opening my mouth widely in order to inhale and exhale felt physi-cally vulnerable, and focusing on my breath meant that I couldn't focus on potential threats. As Kelsey writes in this book, "The inner colonizer is diligently scanning to make sure we're doing things 'the right way.'"

But over the years, Kelsey's profound but practical teachings (now made even more accessible by this book) have helped me to develop both the understanding and rituals that support me as I reconnect with my body, courageously explore the seemingly inhospitable caverns of my body, hold my anxiety with compassion, trust my embodied experience, genuinely rest, say no, take up space, and prioritize my needs too. Further, as I have begun to decolonize my body, I have begun to decolonize my vocational work, thus paving the way for others to get free as well.

We're all too sacred for this. Despite how society has programmed us, we can follow the example of Harriet Tubman and claim our right to be free. In *Decolonizing the Body*, Kelsey Blackwell has generously given us a liberation map. Let's follow it as we learn to trust our inner maps. Let's follow it as we set ourselves free. Let's follow it as we return to set others free.

—Christena Cleveland, PhD
Author of *God Is a Black Woman* and the
founder of the Center for Justice + Renewal

Welcome

I am happy you are here and excited that we get to be in this work together. Though I don't know you, I'm imagining a few things about who you are. I'm imagining that like me, you spend some time feeling the fullness of the world. For as much beauty as you see, there is also so much pain. It's hard to find time to simply be. Do you dream of putting it all down? Do you, like me, try to imagine what liberation would feel like? Would it feel like being part of a humming community, intimately connected yet supported with ample space, time, and ease? Would it feel like tucking your body into something soft, a quiet night, and a good book? Maybe it would feel like riding a bike, hands-free under an audacious sunset sky or contentedly attending to your world alongside busy bumblebees, satisfied in your individual dances and yet fundamentally interwoven.

I'm imagining you spend some time wondering how you can bring more rest, more connection, more love, and more authenticity into your life. Maybe you, like me, bounce between feelings of joyous possibility and waves of grief. Though I don't know you, I feel like I can be honest with you. As though we share the same desire to be who we truly are in our relationships. No masks. No shapeshifting. No pretending.

In this moment, if you were to ask, "How are you?" I would reply that "I am anxious." It's nothing to be alarmed about. My anxiety sits on my chest and radiates up toward my throat. I'm very familiar with these sensations. They've been with me my whole life. There was a time when I tried to push them away, believing they indicated something broken within myself. I've found though that distracting myself or trying to will away what my body is feeling only makes it louder. I've learned to live with my anxiety. Like rain, it moves in and out on its own pattern. Sometimes I can pinpoint a specific reason for the storm. Usually, I cannot. My body is like an antenna that picks up many frequencies. Often what's coming through is a staticky mix of information. There is the steady clarity and insistence of my ancestors, layered with loss, grief, and so much resilience, and there is the fear and righteous rage of our present-day social context. I'm anxious because anxiety is an honest response to tuning in.

Right now, I hope you feel my invitation to show up exactly as you are, and to welcome in all your complexity.

This book is about your radio dial. It is about coming to trust the honesty of your embodied experience. It is also about belonging and community and getting close to the parts of ourselves that have been banished so that we may fully welcome them home. In decolonizing the body, we make a commitment to no longer being afraid of who we are. We know that when we reclaim our bodies, we also support collective transformation.

Please know, the intention of this book is not that you finish these pages and feel complete. Quite the opposite. This is a beginning with no discernible end. Until the systems of oppression that structure our societies are dismantled, we will not be decolonized. Rather, we place ourselves in the stream of the many who have come before and the many who will come after us working toward liberation.

The road ahead is arduous. It is a sticky, muddy path. It is days of toiling forward only to feel (at times) like you're back where you began. You will be frustrated. So why do it? The circuitousness of this route affirms its authenticity. There is no arriving because we've stepped out of linearity—beyond goals, finish lines, and checkboxes—and into the ever-emergent present. In our travels, we're healing the past and seeding the future. There will be moments of satisfaction. The sun will peek out, the rattling of your nervous system will settle, and you'll feel yourself deeply held in the tapestry of creation. Your capacity for attuning to the whispers of the ancestors and guidance from the great beyond will deepen. You will feel in service to life itself. The balm of these moments, the relief of knowing you're right where you're meant to be, anchors you for the unknown ahead. The complexity of this journey brings you to the truth of your being—your decolonized self.

What Is a Colonized Body?

We live under systems of oppression established during colonization. For most bodies of color, if we were to trace our lineage, we would see that at some point, our ancestors were colonized. The reality of what this means is deeply embodied. Colonization is the ripping of children from mothers; the breaking and whipping of backs; the enslavement of bodies; the raping and murdering of women; the annihilation of entire villages; the decimation of culture, language, and foodways. It is bloodied hands and bruised knees for a religion that espouses intolerance. Species are lost, lands destroyed, and entire civilizations erased by the greed and hunger for power that fuel colonization.

Colonization and its sister, imperialism, are the "first poisons" from which other ways of dehumanizing and hierarchically valuing bodies find fertile ground. From this view, it is not just bodies who were violently removed from their land who suffered the impacts of colonization, but also bodies who were stolen, enslaved, and subjugated under colonial value systems. We know we are a colonized people when we do not speak the native tongue of our lineage; when we do not know our lineage; when we do not know our foods, spiritual practices, rituals, and ceremonies; when the social politics that historically governed our people has been erased or consumed by white-value systems. A colonized people are required to adopt the values and traditions of their colonizers to survive. A colonized people do not know where they are from and question their belonging.

As the brutality of colonization spread across the Americas at the beginning in the fifteenth century, how colonizers related to the land is also how they related to the native bodies who inhabited that land. Black and brown bodies were to be controlled and wielded for a specific use. If they did not comply, they were disposed of. While many of our ancestors fought, survival meant contorting to fit the societal role demanded by the dominating power. Writes Frantz Fanon (1952), "Every colonized people— in other words, every people in whose soul an inferiority complex has been created by the death and burial of its local cultural originality—finds itself face to face with the language of the civilizing nation; that is, with the culture of the mother country. The colonized is elevated above his jungle status in proportion to his adoption of the mother country's cultural standards." To do this, our people learned to hold their rage quietly, to not draw attention to themselves, to comply, to attend to the needs of the oppressor, to "keep their heads down." Internally, we learned to push our anger far down, to disconnect from feeling and sensation "to get through," to feel shame for ourselves and our bodies.

These ways of being were taught to us and passed down in our DNA. Today, we feel how this conditioning plays out. A colonized body does not know how to rest; has difficulty saying "no"; may feel guilty for taking up space; may feel more comfortable putting others first and itself last; suspects that it can't rely on anyone; finds it difficult to ask for and receive support; believes it is meant to always be of service, useful, and working; and prioritizes getting ahead over self-connection. The more marginalized social identities one inhabits, for example, being both Black and female-identified, the more likely one is to feel these impacts. We'll explore this in greater depth in chapter 4.

Where Does Decolonizing the Body Come From?

This book is born from my coaching work with women and nonbinary folks of color. These are the themes and practices we've come back to over and over. In weaving the insights from our sessions together, I hope to support the many others holding similar experiences and questions. This book is a reminder that, though your present reality may feel isolating, you are not alone. Unbound by time and space, we stand and breathe alongside you.

I recognize that in my own learning, though many of the practices and approaches I use originate from indigenous communities, several of my teachers and mentors are white bodied. Many times I have asked, How can I decolonize if the lens from which I connect to these teachings is filtered by whiteness? That this is the case is not a surprise given the racial hierarchy we live under in the United States. These are the beings who've been given the social credibility, resources, and visibility to share these tools. Still, I have wanted a purer stream. I've wanted to learn about decolonial somatic practices from the indigenous teachers of my own lineage. I've traced my ancestry hoping that one of my DNA threads would lead me to a wellspring of rituals and practices I could authentically embody. But deepening in the ways of some of my people meant leaving other parts behind.

A true product of the American experiment, my ancestors were both stolen and came of their own volition. DNA testing shows that I am 34.2 percent West African, 10.8 percent Congolese, and 54.3 percent Northwestern European. I also have a trace of Southeast Asian blood. In my studying, the underlying question has always been, Where can 100 percent of me belong? This longing brought me to the dream realm, to my connection to the earth, and to my ancestors. In my fog-soaked sojourns, what always came back was, there is no looking outside for yourself. Your wholeness resides internally. My ancestry is complex, but my completeness is not. I feel gratitude for the many teachers in human, spirit, animal, and plant form who have continually held space and invited trust in the wisdom my body already holds. My call now is to translate these explorations through this politicized Black body, if, for no other reason, than to offer another lens.

Who I Am

I'm a cis, biracial, queer, Black woman. My pronouns are she/her and they/them, and I live on the land of the Ohlone people, now called San Francisco, with my partner and our dog, a rescue pittie–blue heeler, that reminds me constantly of how trauma manifests in the body. I am a partner, daughter, auntie, friend, and bestie. In my professional work, I am a writer and cultural somatics practitioner, mindfulness guide, astrology nerd, and numerologist working alongside powerful, insightful, inspiring, creative, strategic, and thoughtful women of color. I am a lifelong dancer, burgeoning Hoodoo practitioner, Buddhist, bomb-ass chef, and a joiner; I'll say more about that last one shortly. My work is politicized, and I prefer to be in relationships with bodies for whom the words "patriarchy," "colonization," and "racialized capitalism" are not feather-ruffling.

I did not grow up in a politicized household. The words "diversity" and "equity" did not roll off my tongue. My family did not discuss race. My formative years were spent surrounded by whiteness in a small suburb outside of Salt Lake City. My father is Black, my mother is white, and to my peers, I was "weird." My family also isn't Mormon, a faith that centers family gatherings and community activity far beyond the Sunday service. As a teen, I subconsciously tried to minimize my Blackness, shellacking my hair into a tight ponytail and listening to alternative music. I believed that if I wore the right clothes, liked the right things, and spoke the right way, I would fit in. I internalized my inability to belong as something faulty within myself. I learned how to perform what I was "supposed to be": cheerful, friendly, smart, athletic.

I identify as a joiner, someone who loves to be part of a group. I was a Girl Scout. I was in the school choir, a cheerleader, a drama nerd, on the youth city council. I joined the Earth Club yelling alongside others, "Who's your mother!" to baffled neighbors in our small town's homecoming parade. I didn't realize that in all my moving around and jumping in and out of organizations, I was searching for something. My learned skill of becoming who others wanted me to be served me well for being invited in. It did not offer so much in knowing who I was.

I still remember the words of my first meditation instructor: "This practice has made me more who I am than anything else." I didn't know how much I longed for that until I heard it. This was my introduction to Shamatha meditation at the Boulder Shambhala Center, a Buddhist lineage established by Chögyam Trungpa Rinpoche. In that first five-minute session, and many sessions after, I was flooded with anxiety. I couldn't place why or from what, and I was curious. I started to see how my anxiety had been with me for a long time and, like a canary in a coal mine, it told me something honest about my history and my present. I started listening to my body.

This pivotal experience led me to the study of somatics, learning more about the wisdom of my body through the practice of InterPlay and training at the Strozzi Institute. The more I dropped below my head and followed my body, the more myself I felt. I gradually began to make bolder decisions in my work and life. I left Boulder after honestly reflecting on the question, "What does my body want?" The answer was clear: ocean. I moved to the Bay Area and felt for the first time that I could fully be a part of the kind of community I longed for. With willing and dedicated volunteers, I founded a meditation community in Oakland, co-launched a class teaching somatics to artists and activists, published a viral article on the need for BIPOC-only spaces, began teaching somatics in corporate and nonprofit spaces to Black and brown folks, and started coaching women of color to connect to their body's own liberatory wisdom. This work culminated in the online course "Decolonizing the Body," which brings together somatics and spiritual and creative practices for personal and collective liberation.

I tell you all this to help your body discern whether I'm a trustworthy guide. As I mentioned, this journey is about your radio dial. It's about learning to trust what your body is pointing you toward—even when it's uncomfortable. It's about being in the practice of liberation by revealing and reclaiming more of your full self. Take a moment, take a breath, and if you're ready, let's cross this threshold together. I'm happy to have you by my side. I hope you feel me at yours.

Introduction

The impacts of being a colonized people are not always obvious. Maybe you're in a meeting with colleagues, the room is full, and the usual suspects are leading the conversation. You're taking notes and trying to look interested while your head is otherwise occupied. You're thinking about lunch. You're noticing the dynamics in the room. You see how personalities shift depending on who is present. Then you feel it. You don't want to feel it. You try to push it down, distract yourself with a doodle in your notebook and assurance that this will simply go away. It gets worse. The acorn in your throat grows, your heart pounds, and you know your options are clear: you can (a) ignore what you're feeling or (b) follow your gut and say the thing that needs to be said. There's an unspoken truth that's waiting to be recognized. But there's a risk. Others may invalidate your position, dismiss you, or worse.

When this sensation in your body arises, you notice that something else happens too. There's a voice that you hate to admit exists. It says: "If you say anything, you better get it perfect. Speaking means being misunderstood. You will fail. You will look bad. Others will feel sorry for you. They'll be glad it wasn't them. You'll be alone." This voice tries to talk you out of taking a stand. It says: "It's not really that important. Wait until you know more. Let's just see what happens. No one is really going to get you. Everyone will wonder why you're even here. That doesn't really sound smart."

The voice that shows up when your body is indicating that it's time to take up more space, make your needs known, or ask for support is the voice of the colonized self. That voice has one job to do: Keep. You. Small. It wants to keep you small so you keep doing what *it* wants you to do. This voice was forged by the multiheaded Hydra that encompasses the colonial project.

This is the voice of white supremacy.

This is the voice of the patriarchy.

This is the voice of racialized capitalism.

This is the voice of transphobia.

If that voice is here now, even if it's just a faint whisper saying, "This isn't going to work for you," know that the mere fact that it's here indicates that you're in the right place. Our time together is about learning to trust and follow the guidance of what your body is pulling you toward in the face of all the pressures that suggest the opposite. That voice is showing up because it's scared that you're going to do something to diminish its power.

Do You Know This Person?

She's smart and driven. At her job, she's the first to pick up extra work during a crunch. Her boss relies on her, maybe a little too much, to go above and beyond. She knows she's killing it, but on some level, she also knows the hustle is killing her. The lines between work and home life are blurry. Time that could be spent unplugging and resting are instead spent planning and reviewing or numbing out in front of a screen. She'd like to take some time for herself, to really nourish and connect, but there's always just one…more…thing.

If you find it difficult to rest, if you find that your mind is always going a mile a minute and it's hard to turn it off, this person might be you. There's nothing wrong with being on your game. Go ahead and get that paper. The problem arises when you realize you have only one speed for navigating through life: go! Slowing down is hard if not impossible. Vacation? What's that? It may feel like you're just not wired to unwind. If this were true though, the longing for another kind of life would evaporate. You would be satisfied. If you're hungry for more peace, this is an indication that it *is* possible. Rather than simply not having the capacity to "not do," something else is at play.

We are physically and energetically shaped by the environments we live in. In embodiment work, we call this your "somatic shape." Your shape is essentially your go-to practices and ways of being for navigating life. It includes your "embodiment of beliefs, resilience and survival strategies, habits, and actions," writes Staci Haines in *The Politics of Trauma* (2019). Your shape is informed by where you live, your family dynamics, the community you grew up in, the institutions you engage with, social norms, political and historical forces, and your relationship to spirit and the earth. Your shape is why it may feel like your mind is always on turbo-drive and why it's difficult to slow down, take care of your body, and be fully present with those you love. Systems of oppression have a direct impact on our shape. Because of the speed required to sustain capitalism and white supremacy, many bodies of color are shaped to believe that we can prove our worth by doing "enough." It's hard to put down the projects that are always before us and simply enjoy being where we are. This shaping has colonial roots. In decolonizing the body, we're shifting our somatic shape to be more aligned with what really matters to us.

Unpacking the Colonial Project

The colonial project undergirds the fabric of the societies we live in. How is it possible that colonization, an event most of us have not actively lived through, could still be impacting our lives and bodies? Because the values of colonialism, and the arrogance it requires to exact its purpose, are still very much in place. Consider, what might be needed for men to enact genocide against indigenous bodies, plunder the land, and destroy native plants and animals for amusement, profit, and pleasure? Whatever was going on inside these historical "conquerors," is it so very different from what is operating in those who obliterate Black and brown bodies, erase queer and trans bodies, refuse gun reform laws, frack the earth, and poison the oceans? As colonization requires a disconnection from the body in those who perpetuate its aims, so too does white supremacy, racialized capitalism, and transphobia. One could easily write volumes about how these systems overlap and support each other. For our purposes, an overview will suffice. For a list of books, podcasts, and videos to deepen your study, see the Resources at the back of this book.

The Language of Domination

Let's start with some terminology. You've likely heard these words and have a sense of what they mean, but let's define them so we're on the same page.

Colonization. Colonization is the act of an external power asserting authority over a group of people and their lives, land, and natural resources. Settler colonialism is the forceful establishment of settlements via the elimination, subjugation, and assimilation of the original inhabitants. Practices in settler colonialism included the genocide of indigenous bodies, the establishment of reservations, and forced enrollment into boarding schools, citizenship, and Christianity.

Imperialism. Though they are not the same, "imperialism" is often used interchangeably with "colonialism." Through imperialism, a country builds its empire by extending power over other countries and territories via military might and economic coercion. Imperialism happens without colonialism when the invading country does not send settlers. The US's domination of American Samoa, Guam, the US Virgin Islands, Puerto Rico, and the Northern Mariana Isands is an example.

Racial capitalism. Racial capitalism points to the inseparability of capitalism and racism. Capitalism as an economic system requires a perpetual accumulation of resources at an increasing rate. Because perpetual extraction and accumulation are not sustainable, the system relies on relationships of inequality to maintain itself. Historically and in present day, that primary differentiator of human value is the color of one's skin. Racial capitalism requires the labor of Black and brown bodies to create and concentrate wealth for the predominately white plutocratic few.

Transphobia. The belief in a gender binary and discrimination against bodies that don't conform to "traditional" gender roles. Transphobia can include an aversion to trans people, refusal to use preferred pronouns, overall negative beliefs about trans people, and irrational fears about trans people.

White supremacy. Seeded by European colonists, white supremacy is the belief that people with "white" skin are superior to all others. To establish harmony and order, white bodies must dominate and control Black and brown bodies. This happens via genocide, enslavement, and forced acculturation.

The Program

Throughout these pages, you'll see references to "the program." The program is shorthand for the juggernaut that is the colonialist-imperialist-white supremacist-capitalist patriarchy. Using the term "the program" also conveys that this is a script we've learned. The tenets that shape these systems are not innate; they are distortions of humanity's fundamental nature to live harmoniously. If collaboration were not instinctive, none of us would be here now. Humans are not the strongest species nor the fastest or most fearsome. It is our ability to work together that has allowed us to survive. The further we get from living cooperatively, the closer we come to our own extinction. All around, we see the societal impacts of our indoctrination by the program. We're plagued by income inequality, political polarization, racial injustice, gun violence, food insecurity, an increasingly warming planet, and more.

The program believes "winning" is an individual pursuit. We're meant to battle each other to obtain the most wealth, the most power, the most influence, the most beauty, the most success, and so on. The program is fed by a desire for domination. The program influences all. It is at the foundation of the structures and systems that colonized the Western world. It seeks every opening to reassert itself—even in spaces dedicated to its undoing. This happens due to external pressures that lead us to abandon our values in favor of productivity and efficiency. We're all intended to fulfill one role within the program: to keep its control in place by fighting each other for resources. Not matter how much "wealth" we attain, we never truly feel secure.

Under the program, we're taught to believe that:

Power is hierarchical

Power is a zero-sum game

The earth's resources are for the taking

Nature should remain at the margin

Whiteness is the standard

One's humanity is up for valuation

Some bodies are disposable

Individualism wins over the collective

Interdependence does not exist

Identity operates on a binary

Financial wealth reflects human worth

Happiness comes from material consumption.

What else? What other collective beliefs and values are rooted in the program?

Internalizing the Program

Our bodies are shaped by the program. The program would have us believe that we are fundamentally unworthy. We are meant to work harder and harder to be "enough." We strive to be enough at work, enough for our families, enough for our friends, enough for people we don't even know, but trust in this enoughness remains out of grasp. We doubt our contributions. When our bodies try to show us something else—sensations that indicate we need rest, for example—we make them the problem. We learn to relate to our bodies as issues to be fixed. And when we simply don't have time to deal with their aches and pains, we stop feeling altogether.

By internalizing the program, we learn to:

Disconnect from feeling

Disconnect from the body

Operate from the neck up

Prioritize speed and productivity

Not need others

Fear mistakes

Take on too much responsibility

Relate to others as competition

Fear the unknown.

We're shown that this is how we must be to "make it" and attain "success." Organizing ourselves in this way proves our humanity in the eyes of the program. The harder we drive ourselves, the more "human" we become. Stepping out of line from this expectation not only positions us as less than, but also puts our body in jeopardy. We become a threat and disposable. It is no coincidence that internalizing the program fundamentally disconnects us from our bodies and hence the location of our true power.

Because we were born into the program and fed its values since birth, our internalization of it can feel like who we are. We may doubt there's anything that can help us find the rest and peace we seek until we "win" by the rules of the systems that oppress us. Our internalized oppression drives us to amass enough resources so we don't have to do anything for anyone anymore. But our hunger for this freedom remains the provenance of dreams. The system wasn't designed for us to win. We toil and worry, but we never arrive. There is another way.

The Role of Somatics

When we intentionally connect to the body, we access a wisdom stream of support that challenges the narrow lens of the program. Our bodies become guides leading us back to a more complete existence. By engaging in values-aligned, body-centered practices, we gradually unhook from the delusions perpetuated by the program that drive us to try to "earn" our humanity. Instead, we begin to embody the truth: we are fundamentally whole and worthy as we are.

Practices that suggest the body is a pathway toward understanding our intrinsic enoughness are called "somatic." You'll see this word throughout the book. "Soma" is a Greek term that means "the living organism in its wholeness." The practice of somatics is an integration of all our parts. The soma includes the mind, body, and spirit and incorporates in our learning how to trust and follow bodily sensations, thinking, feeling, and emotions.

As we feel for what's underneath the conditioning of the program, we access our embodied history—our shaping. In bringing somatics to the journey of decolonization, we're inviting the body to guide us in remembering our indigeneity; reclaiming our power; releasing old patterns; and relating to the phenomenal world as interconnected and fundamentally supportive of life. We're also centering practices that prioritize rest, ritual, and community.

Your Lineage Lives in You

My grandmother was the daughter of a sharecropper from Arkansas, a petite woman as sweet as the syrupy Kool-Aid she made for me and my eleven cousins. Learning of her upbringing was like trying to gather sand with a sieve. Her father was a farmer who "grew all sorts of things" and "moved around a lot." I knew that Grammy helped raise her siblings when her mother died in childbirth. That's it. She didn't talk of the past.

When our family came together for holidays, after the meal, Grammy pulled a sheet out and used it to cover the dishes and platters on the dining table. Rather than doing dishes, she would say, "Let's enjoy each other." Grammy didn't want us to worry about doing. She wanted her grandchildren to know a childhood freedom I suspect she never had. She had a knack for knowing how to simply be. Many nights, even with the commotion of connection around, she would lie back on her brown couch and close her eyes. "Grammy, are you sleeping?" one of us would ask. "No Honey, I'm just resting my eyes."

Our bodies are connected to a knowing that extends back, back, back before these systems of oppression were ever forged. It is in our bodies that we contact our intuition and our innate human needs to move toward rest, nutritive connection, and expression. In our body, we first attune to environments where something is "off." It tells us, "Hey, pay attention here," or "Hey, get out of here." Decolonizing the body is not a practice of putting something on to reconnect to this essential wisdom, but rather an orientation toward taking something off. We're throwing off the colonial overcoats we've been buried in and reclaiming what we've always known. We're allowing ourselves to "rest our eyes" and simply trust what our body is communicating. This is a practice of re-membering ourselves.

Two Kinds of Remembering

Imagine a black bird flying through the sky. As the sun glints off its feathers, you see a rainbow of color: red, purple, green, blue, orange. The bird flies high and straight, but something is unique about it. Though it is flying forward, its head is turned back over its body. In its mouth, it holds an egg.

This is a Sankofa bird. It knows the way forward because it carries with it the wisdom of the past. In fact, the only way it's able to fly toward the future is because of its commitment to staying connected to what is behind. *Sankofa* is the shortened proverb, "*Se wo were fi na wosankofa a yenkyi,*" from the Akan language of Ghana, which is translated as, "Go back and fetch it." It is a reminder to African people that the way forward requires staying in touch with the traditions of our past.

The program functions through two kinds of dismemberment: it makes us forget the power and wisdom of our own bodies, and it erases the dignity of our ancestors. If the program is dismemberment, we meet it with Sankofa: remembering. Remembering means reconnecting with our own physical bodies (*re-membering*) as well as the wisdom of our people (*remembering*).

A few years ago, OkayAfrica TV did a segment on Erykah Badu as she received DNA results of her ancestry. (See Resources for the link to view it.) After swabbing her cheek and sending it to African Ancestry, Badu discovered that her lineage on her mother's side can be traced to the Bamileke people in the grassland region of Cameroon. As she receives this news, an elder from the community welcomes her and she is given a *toghu*, a finely embroidered red, gold, and black garment traditionally worn during times of celebration and ceremony. She reflects later that, "being able to single out exactly where my ancestors walked, what we smelled, what we heard, and what attracts us—the colors and the fabrics—these are the things that I vibrate toward naturally." She then adds, "There's one call I do on stage, *lulululululululu*. This happens to be also the call of the tribe. So, some things are just in us" (Okayplayer 2014).

It is via *re-membering,* or connecting with the intelligence that lives below the head, that we are able to remember the wise ways of our ancestors. Though we may not conceptually know where our people are from, they are, as Badu says, alive in us.

Who This Books Is For

Operating counter to the ways that the program suggests is risky. This truth is particularly true for queer and fem-identified bodies of color. The threats to our well-being, the ways we're asked to be the bridge, take care of, hold space for, stand up to, shut down…being a body of color is a contortion act. In all that flexing, it is our connection to ourselves that gets lost. This book is for us. Please note, I use the words "woman," "women," and "she, her, and hers" throughout this text. I am including all fem-identifying people in my use of these identifiers. Additionally, I believe that people of color of any gender may be well served by this book.

If you're not a Black or brown person, you are welcome to read this book, but know that it was not written for you. May these words spark curiosity and deeper inquiry about what it means to live as a racialized body in this time. Perhaps some of what is shared will resonate with you. If so, I'm happy for the support it offers.

How to Use This Book

In the tradition of numerology, the number four represents foundation. It is the number from which stability can arise. There are, for example, four seasons, four elements, four chambers of the heart, four sections in a Native American medicine wheel, and four immeasurable truths. This book is also comprised of four parts: "Re-Member," "Reclaim," "Release," and "Relate." Within each section are two chapters, each with a myth of colonization countered by a decolonizing truth.

These pages weave together storytelling, conceptual learning, practice, and reflection. Because our journey is primarily somatic, we'll reconnect with the body through feeling, moving, settling, stretching, sensing, and being. Notice I did not say "reading" here. We are in a paradox. How do we do this work through a book? The answer lies in the practices between the words. If you simply *read* this book without *doing* this book, you won't get a lot out of it. You may find the perspective and approach interesting, but this is simply looking at the recipe. To enjoy the meal, one must get in the kitchen. The kitchen is alive. It is where we smell the sweet smokiness of the paprika, feel the steam from the bubbling pot on our face, taste a bit on the back of our hand, and offer a little more of this and that. The savoring that comes from this work is accessed when we let the thinking body fall away and arrive at feeling. I'll be with you through written and guided embodied exercises. Audio versions of some practices are available at the website for this book, http://www.newharbinger.com/50614. I also suggest dedicating a journal specifically to the reflections you'll find in these pages.

The Necessity of Risk

This work requires stepping into the unknown. Unhooking from the program means confronting forces intent on keeping us from doing just that. These pressures are both internal and external. Externally, our needs are challenged and dismissed. Because we live in a society in which the program holds dominance, it is not always safe to combat its authority. When our lives are on the line, we take care of ourselves in whatever ways are needed to protect our safety.

The risk I'm suggesting here is not about putting ourselves in harm's way. Rather, the risk we take is in discerning when more freedom is possible and taking a chance to lean into it. What are you willing to risk to honor the lives of your ancestors? What are you willing to risk for a more liberated existence? What are you willing to risk so that future generations may experience more freedom? By turning to the breath and the beating of your heart, you get the first internal feeling that something more, something truer is possible. There are faint whispers…whispers that at first seem impossible. Unheeded, they get louder. Then comes the choice. Turn toward this wild beating and gut-knowing? Or push it down? Ignore it? This book aims to support you in taking the unpredictable yet more alive choice—the choice that connects you with the fullness of who you are.

An Aspiration

If you don't know, look up the name of the indigenous people who inhabited the land you are now on. You will need their names for what is to come. Here is a good resource: https://native-land.ca/.

You can repeat the following words or let them wash over you.

Sweet Mother Earth, she who supports all with generous abundance, without you, there is nothing. Even in our negligence, you continue to sustain us. May we wake up to care for you with the same attention you unwaveringly offer. May our roots extend down into the soil, and as they do so, may we come into contact with the stories that have been buried—our own and those of the places we inhabit.

Original caretakers of this land (speak the names of the indigenous people who inhabited the land you are now on), may we always recognize and speak your name. May we deeply know that wherever we are, the land that holds us was not discovered. May we see that despite the hollow left by the disposal, enslavement, and subjugation of native people, you have not been erased. You live and breathe among us. May we reembody the tradition of care and reciprocity between earth, beings, and humans that extends back.

To our own humble vessels, may we release ourselves from shame and guilt as we peel back how our bodies adapted to survive inside of systemic oppression. May we hold the complexity that, though perhaps distant, all people at some time were indigenous. As Black and brown bodies for whom this identity is more contactable, may we hold our role in societal healing as that of coming back into right relationship with the life-giving wisdom that resides in our bones. Alongside the Great Mother, may we relate to our own bodies as altars. Ase.

PART I

Re-Member

It's a heavy door. A door that requires many bodies to open. But with enough, you can just crack it. At first, the light is intimidatingly bright. You shield your face against it and consider going back to the safety of the machine. But then you sense it: Life. Earth. Water. The world humans were meant to live in.

CHAPTER 1

How Are You?

*People get used to anything. The less you think about your oppression,
the more your tolerance for it grows. After a while, people just think
oppression is the normal state of things. But to become free, you have to
be acutely aware of being a slave.*

—Assata Shakur

I remember the first time I heard Dr. Maya Angelou speak. I was thirteen
years old and actively trying to erase my racial identity. I wanted straight
blonde hair. I wanted blue eyes. I wanted to be white. This was the era of
grunge—oversized flannel and baggy jeans. The clothes enveloped me in
a way that suited how I felt inside: small, unseen, and unimportant. I was
crouched in a stadium seat, my legs propped on the chair in front of me,
further accentuating my turtlelike shape.

Dr. Angelou took her time walking to the podium. She wore a head-
dress and a long flowing print. She was taller than I expected, and she did
not shrink her size. In fact, just the opposite. She held her head upright and
regal. When she arrived at the microphone, she did not immediately
address us. She spent several breaths taking in her audience—a sea of
white faces—the faintest smile on her lips. I felt myself sinking lower in my
plastic seat. She and I, as far as I could see, were the only ones like us in
the amphitheater. I was embarrassed by her unapologetic Blackness, by
how much space she took up. I was sure the audience would start laughing
at any moment. I wanted to invisibilize both her and myself.

Then she spoke. Looking back, it was just as she says, "People will
forget what you said, people will forget what you did, but people will never

forget how you made them feel." I don't remember what she recited. I remember that she held herself as though she knew she possessed the most precious gift. She was delighted by the joy we were surely experiencing in receiving it. I felt myself drawn in, magnetized by the golden web of her words and presence. When she concluded, I felt proud to share something with this woman: to, for the first time, be Black. In spite of the unfamiliar or embarrassing versions of Blackness I'd seen in the media, here was an example of the dignity and cultural wealth of *my* people. I had never seen a Black woman so fully self-possessed. I didn't start wearing headdresses, but I did walk out of that stadium a little taller.

This story highlights a fundamental aspect of colonization. A colonized people are disconnected from the rich cultural history from which they stem. Through centuries of lies and misinformation, we're made to feel ashamed about our bodies and where we come from. We're told our people did not contribute anything of note to society. They were primitive and simple. We are shown that assimilating and adapting to whiteness is the path to acceptance and success.

This sense of being faulty is able to color not just our appraisal of our external appearance but also how we feel inside. When our anxiety peaks for seemingly no reason, we're wrong. The doubt we feel before we make a request is wrong. Even our depression over the state of the world is wrong.

What Dr. Angelou showed me so many years ago is that walking with dignity while not adhering to the values of whiteness is possible. In fact, reclaiming who we are in the face of pressures demanding we conform to some narrow definition of acceptability makes us powerful beyond measure. Where do we begin? By asking ourselves a simple question: How am I?

Feeling for Your How

How are you? Really, take a moment to ask yourself. How are you in this moment? If your answers is "fine" or "good," probe more deeply. Sometimes these pat responses are ways we've been trained to look past ourselves. How are you sleeping? How are you eating? How is your mood? How is your energy?

When we check in with ourselves, we create an opening for sensing what is true. While some of what we notice may feel pleasurable, often (given the intensity of late-stage capitalism) what we feel is not so great. We're tired. We're anxious. We're distracted. In my work, I've noticed a pattern when I ask this question to clients. Many folks leave their bodies behind when answering it. They say things like *okay* or *meh*. My follow-up question is always, "What is happening *in your body* that indicates that to you?"

I ask the same to you: *How are you in your body? How is it feeling to inhabit your skin?*

These straightforward (though understandably complex) questions are the beginning of interrupting the program. They are where we can start to see what scripts are unconsciously running in us and make a decision to arrive in the present moment. There's so much power in the present moment. In this moment, right...*here* is where you decide to make choices that align with what really matters to you. It is where you decide if you want to rest your body or keep going, to venture forth with more of who you are or not. In the present moment, we get to see and question the patterns our colonized selves would prefer we stick to.

Some of this may be happening for you right now, or none of it may. Maybe you're realizing, "You know what? I'm uncomfortable in this chair; let me adjust." Or maybe, "Hmm...I don't think I'm up for reading in this moment; let me come back to this."

Whatever is or is not arising, there's one final piece that's important when assessing your how. Please remind yourself that there's nothing you *have to* fix in this moment. If you can, offer yourself and your body some kindness.

That Chatty Colonized Self

The colonized self is not too happy with the prospect of assessing how you are. This part of ourselves is freaked out by the possibility that we might be feeling discomfort and not *immediately* make a plan to banish these sensations. If some version of this is showing up for you now, this is a lovely opportunity to get to know this voice. Notice, how does it speak to you? What is its tone? Is it urgent? Does it want you to put rules around something? Is it tsk-tsking you for not doing it right? If this voice is here, can you pause before believing it? Before acting on it? Perhaps, can you take a breath?

Our colonized self is the part of us that is shaped by the program. It holds unconscious beliefs and patterns that keep us behaving in the "correct" way, aka adhering to the role society has set for us. For bodies of the global majority, this means striving toward (or appearing to be striving toward) the values of white dominance while not challenging white bodies' access to resources or power.

In order to do this, we must disconnect from our bodies. This disconnection has two parts: we're expected to shave off or modify the parts of ourselves that are too "much," aka ethnic, and we're meant to literally stop feeling and assume a kind of plastic appeasability that's of no apparent harm and eager to be of service. If we don't take on some version of this, we are challenged. We learn to disconnect from our bodies because doing so helps us survive inside this inhospitable environment. The pain of this—feeling that aspects of ourselves are intrinsically wrong—further leads us to avoid attuning to what's going on below the neck.

An Internal Tug-of-War

Our decolonized self coexists with the parts of us that have been conditioned by the program. This small voice is what often leads us to long to be more fully ourselves. Perhaps you see the patterns you're done adhering to? You're tired of pleasing and putting everyone before yourself. Maybe you sense that your body is communicating with you but don't know how to discern its messages, or perhaps you're just ready for a deeper connection to your body.

When our decolonized and colonized selves are operating within us, it can feel like an internal tug-of-war. The inner colonizer is diligently scanning to make sure we're doing things "the right way." It's been trained since birth to do this and is often really good at it. It believes that the only way to stay safe is by playing by all the rules. At the same time, the decolonized self is continually communicating how to be true to yourself. Your heart pounds, your stomach drops, your gut quivers. It says things like, "I'm tired of this." "What if I just said no?" "Something is off."

The sensations that co-arise with sentiments pushing you to reclaim your agency are the body's way of reminding you who you are. The body is pointing you toward how to access more of yourself. But unaccustomed to noticing and following these sensations, the mind (the colonized self's most important player) leaps in. It interrupts the language of the decolonized self as "dangerous" or "incorrect" and plays over its messages with thoughts like, *That's selfish. What's the big deal? Just do it. You better not fuck this up.*

As our inner colonizer and decolonized selves do their jobs, we feel at odds within ourselves. There's an inner push-pull that makes us feel like our own worst enemy. We self-flagellate for holding ourselves back, all the while reifying the very patterns that hold us as continually deficient. We double down on our "self-improvement" plans. We overwork ourselves. We check out.

The conditioned self wants to protect us from reclaiming ourselves because history and our own epigenetics have shown us that it's often not safe to claim our full agency in relationship with privileged bodies who hold power. And while that is true, the problem is that our conditioned self is a little too good at its role. It goes into overdrive to keep us perpetually in check. This inner watchdog drives us to adopt embodied patterns that become generalized as how we simply "do life." We hold our breath. We make ourselves physically smaller. We focus all our attention on our thinking self and forget we have bodies. Again, this all makes sense. We don't live in a world where it is safe to have a Black or brown body. These adaptations have successfully kept us from being harmed. The problem is, these contortions are not who we are, and over time, we begin to feel it.

Asking ourselves *how we are* and allowing the multitude of what comes forward—even if it's inconvenient, nonsensical, messy, or eerily quiet—is the first step toward validating what the body knows. Attuning to your *how* gives you an opportunity to feel for all that is at play. With that awareness comes more choice. Rather than being run by the program, we can become the arbiters of what is right for us. In subsequent chapters, we'll explore exactly how one might do this. For now, simply notice, again, How am I?

Keeping Us Distracted

The best way to keep us from feeling our *how* is to keep busy. Sometimes I imagine the program as a blacked-out warehouse filled with treadmills. We're all in the warehouse. We were born there and immediately plopped on a machine. The speed of our treadmill is set by society. Person of color? That's immediately an increase of three ticks. Woman? Add another two. Gender nonbinary, differently abled, poor? Tick, tick, tick. In front of us is the thrilling possibility of success. Success is happiness, freedom, nice things. To get there, we must not only keep up with the pace society has set for us but exceed it. We punch up the belt ever faster, believing this is the key to eventually getting off. Around us, we see the faces of others on their treadmills. Everyone is trying to keep it together. To look confident. We don't see how fast their legs are scurrying underneath. Some aren't making it. They're tripping, getting ground by the gears. We look away. Their experience points to the truth. One wrong step and it could be you.

So we run. We're taught that any inability to do this is *our* fault. The white able-bodied men, they're on a treadmill too. We can't be sure how fast their pace is set, though they tell us it's very fast. They're the only ones who boast about this.

The location of the warehouse is key. Inside, it is an abyss. Floating treadmills in space. It never occurs to us to get off. Getting off would surely mean plummeting endlessly into a deep void toward a painful death. We don't have time to see there's a door. It's a heavy door. A door that requires many bodies to open. But with enough, you can just crack it. At first the light is intimidatingly bright. You shield your face against it and consider going back to the safety of the machine. But then you sense it: Life. Earth. Water. The world humans were meant to live in.

The program is the mechanism by which we've been taught to disconnect from what is life-giving. This includes the wisdom of the earth, the wisdom of our bodies, and the wisdom of our interconnection. The program turns out the lights and puts us all on treadmills to feed its survival.

"If we beat the system at its own game, we've lost," reminds author and teacher Báyò Akómoláfé. "It is no longer time to rush through the contested world blinded by fury and anger—however worthwhile these are. Now, we think, is the time to 'retreat' into the real work of reclamation, to re-member again our humanity through the intimacy of our relationships. The time is very urgent—we must slow down." (Akómoláfé n.d.).

We must risk getting off the treadmill.

Myth of Colonization: Who I Am Is What I Do

What is the best way to distract people from accessing their how? By keeping them so busy that they don't have time to notice or take care of what is happening in their body, by making them believe that what they produce is the only way to garner respect for and keep their body safe.

In the perversion of the program, we believe having a body means working to control our body. It's a mechanism to transport our head. We're expected to tamp down whatever is messy or doesn't fit. We're expected to get it to fit a certain shape and size. We're expected to always be ten steps ahead of our body—preparing for the threat that is always around the corner.

The most efficient way to conform to this expectation is to internally cede power to our thinking minds. This is the strategizing, future-oriented part of ourselves. Our thinking brain becomes like a dictator wielding *power over* our other sensibilities. Author and teacher Starhawk (1989) defines power-over relationships in her book *Truth or Dare: Encounters with Power, Authority, and Mystery.* "We are so accustomed to power over, so steeped in its language and its implicit threats, that we often become aware of its functioning only when we see its extreme manifestations," she writes. Power over is the power of the program. It relies on force, coercion, and control to move its agenda along, and it influences through fear. Power over is what is operating when we're running on the treadmill.

It's not that our brains are the villains. They're simply fulfilling the role they were assigned. However, in decolonizing the body, we recognize that this strategizing, analytical, future-oriented part of ourselves is better suited for another job: *power with* the body. *Power with* is power that builds from collaboration and relationship. It is trust in sensation, making space for the unknown, honoring emotion, inclusion, navigating with vulnerability, connection to spirit, connection to joy, and aliveness. While the body tells us what is truly up, the head can help us trust and take actions that align with that. How do we get there? We can start by assessing our how.

Decolonizing Truth: Who I Am Is How I Am

The best way to assess your how is through ongoing practice, by repeatedly taking a moment to tune in and ask yourself: *How am I?* This awareness is the foundation for interrupting the mind and its power-over authority and building a relationship to power *with*. Knowing your how gives you options.

This isn't the way most of us have been trained to relate to our mind and body. With the mind in the driver's seat, we bounce from one thing to the next. The program has taught us that we must *do* to prove our value. In decolonizing, we recognize that we *already* have value. There's nothing we must do to affirm this. Don't worry if your knowing of this doesn't feel accessible right now. This is the journey we are on. The first step is engaging in the opposite of what we've been trained to do. We slow down so we can make an honest assessment of *how* we are. We'll explore this in more detail in the next chapter. For now, let's look more closely at the differences between a body that is defined by *what* it does versus *how* it is. Take note of anything that is familiar to you.

A body that is *what* it does (colonized):	A body that is *how* it is (decolonizing):
Finds it difficult to truly rest	Protects time for recharging and rest
Does not have time to heal	Takes time to care for itself when needed
Focuses on flaws in the mirror	Offers kindness in the mirror
Is oppressed by strict diets and exercise regimes	Eats and exercises for pleasure and well-being
Shuts down feeling (no time for that)	Allows and takes care of feelings as they arise
Feels shame for not "keeping up"	Realizes "keeping up" or "being behind" is the language of the program
Numbs itself to "unwind"	Notices when the body needs rest before burning out
Feels imprisoned by time and rigid schedules	Realizes we shape our relationship to time
Is organized in a me-against-the-world mentality	Relies on relationships and interconnection to weather difficulty
Feels like a fraud	Knows feeling like a fraud is an impact of white dominance; offers gentleness
Must keep it together	Offers self-compassion
Feels shame that it doesn't conform to a certain body size and shape	Celebrates its form; realizes that to have a body is to be in constant change

The Importance of Practice

Throughout these pages, you'll see many opportunities to practice. You practice to move this learning from the conceptual realm into the body. What does your body know about what we're exploring? What does it say? Like learning any language, it takes time to understand what the body is indicating, but with patience and care, you can discern more and more. These practices are simple but don't yield all their wisdom after one experience. They're meant to be done over and over again. And each time you do them, you may have a new insight, a new understanding that until that moment remained under the surface.

A saying I love in the somatic lineage I practice is, "You are what you practice, and you're always practicing something." The question then becomes, Is what you're practicing aligned with what really matters to you? Practice is how you shift from believing your value rests solely in the boxes you're able to check to understanding you are more than the sum of your accomplishments. Rather than approaching these practices like items on your to-do list or things to complete to be a "good student," I suggest considering them as opportunities to explore your how. Is your body drawn to this exercise? What does it need? Like brushing the beach from a delicate sand dollar, can you engage with a sense of unhurried and gentle discovery?

SOMATIC PRACTICE: Let It Out with a Sigh

This practice is simply taking a deep breath. You can do this practice anytime, as often as you like. You can also listen to a guided audio version of this practice at http://www.newharbinger.com/50614.

Let yourself feel the points of your body making contact with support.

Take a deep breath and let it out with an audible sigh.

Do this three times, seeing if you can extend the length and volume of the sigh each time.

Notice.

Throughout these pages, you'll see invitations for a somatic pause. You can do this by engaging in what you just practiced—the "Let It Out with a Sigh." This pause is a little space to digest what you've read by noticing what is happening in your body, your how.

Why We Notice

After any somatic practice, you will always be asked to notice. When you notice, you're building a bridge between the feeling self and the thinking self. There's no pressure to arrive at something profound when you notice. You may, but this isn't about big takeaways. Rather, you're indicating to yourself (and sometimes to others) that what the body is experiencing is important and worthy of paying attention to. There's also no need to try to make sense of what you notice. Just allow whatever is coming up to come up. Sometimes the connections between what you're noticing and your daily life come together much later.

What are you noticing after doing the above exercise? In noticing, check in with what is happening in your body, thoughts, sensations, and feelings. Keep track of what you're noticing from this practice in a journal designated for this journey.

In the next chapter, we'll explore how accessing your *how* with regularity is an essential practice for unhooking from the pressures of the program, and I'll introduce an approach to guide your way.

CHAPTER 2

Slowing Down

What if we could release ourselves from an internalized time clock and remember that slow is efficient, slow is effective, slow is beautiful?

—Alexis Pauline Gumbs

What is the pace of the program? Remember, "the program" is shorthand for the colonialist-imperialist-white-supremacist-capitalist-patriarchal society we live in. How has that pace seeped into our Black and brown bodies? What is our collective relationship with time? I cleared a week to explore these questions, and then I got sick. During what was supposed to be hours of interruption-free productivity, I slept on the couch, a box of tissues nearby, intermittently reading, dozing, and watching TV. I felt the undercurrent of tension that arises when things do not go as I've planned. Of course I was sick.

In my preparations, I'd been burning incense, pulling cards, offering to my ancestors, and asking for wisdom to guide my words. Their midwifery showed up right on time. I imagined my tall and dignified Big Mamma standing in front of me chuckling, "Come on girl, it's time to be about what you're talking about." While worry and uncertainty swirled in my head, each sneeze, wadding of tissue, and wrapping into blankets brought me back down to feeling, to sensation, and to the reminder of how to trust and take care of my body when my head wants something entirely different.

Our bodies know how to slow down. They know how to rest and take care of themselves. They know that this, more than anything, must come first. Sometimes we just need a little help getting out of our own way.

Another Kind of Nourishment

If we are *how* we are, how do we unplug from the program and allow ourselves to move at a pace that centers care and well-being? This, in many ways, is the challenge of our technological age. I liken this hunger for rest to the gnaw our bodies feel when they are calling for actual sustenance. The ache builds, but maybe we're too busy to address it. Maybe we don't know what to eat. Maybe life is moving so fast that we don't recognize the need is there until we're ravenous. The body demands something, *anything*. Those chocolate-covered pretzels begin to look pretty tantalizing. Some part of us may be none too pleased with this choice, but screw it. We distractedly consume whatever is closest until the fire is somewhat quelled. All the while we keep going.

I don't have anything against salty, crispy, sugary deliciousness. In fact, I love these foods. But while convenience is certainly craveable, it isn't satiating. It doesn't offer our body what it needs to be truly sustained. To be nourished means giving ourselves real food, you know, vegetables, protein, and complex carbs, so we can function. The same can be said for our need for real, nutritive rest.

The body's need for slowness is the same as its need for good food. While we will eventually, hopefully get a nourishing meal, the verdict remains out for quality downtime. By quality downtime, I mean time easing into the rhythm of the day and allowing its ebbs and flows to guide us, when any open space is not immediately filled with doing, when we can allow ourselves a moment of pleasure without worry that we'll pay some price on the other side, when we can be unburdened from the pressure to be continually efficient and productive, and instead simply be. Not only do we not get enough of this time, we've collectively been trained to fear it. Writes Jenny Odell (2019), "To capitalist logic, which thrives on myopia and dissatisfaction, there may indeed be something dangerous about something as pedestrian as doing nothing: escaping laterally toward each other, we might just find that everything we wanted is already here."

I'm fascinated by this idea of "escaping laterally." How I interpret it is that "escape," or our ability to rest and connect with pleasure, doesn't require booking a beachside vacation or even diligently carving out time to be left alone. In fact, compartmentalizing downtime as something we "earn" is antithetical to what many of us are seeking when we make these plans. By relegating pleasure to a cordoned-off area, we play into the capitalist narrative that all other time must be virtuously spent proving ourselves worthy of such a break. Instead, we can schedule time off *and* we can regularly nourish ourselves by, as Odell suggests, lateral escape.

When we escape laterally, we take a moment to put the to-do list down and extend our awareness out. We allow ourselves to arrive fully in our *how,* in the present moment. We notice, for example, the curl of steam from our morning cup of coffee, the rhythm of neighbors ebbing and flowing, the soft snore of our partner, the gentle decay of the backyard fence, the drawn-out angle of late fall shadows. Our body settles. Amid this, the ping of rolling emails, the looming deadlines, and last-minute vacation deals no longer have the same hold over us. They are demoted from being dictators of our time to simply things among the milieu of so many others. By escaping laterally, we slow down enough to recognize we have choices. We can begin to divorce ourselves from letting our schedules be run by outside forces. Rather than having our well-being contingent on what we do, we instead find it in the fullness of our lives as they exist.

Our bodies require lateral escape. We need this respite to make sense of our days. We need it to integrate and reflect. We need it to understand our world and our place in it. Without these kinds of moments of presence, the impact of our go, go, go lifestyles adds up. We feel a weariness in our eyes and a tightness across our shoulders. Our sleep is unsatisfying. We get sick. A malaise of fatigue drags behind us like a leaden ball.

SOMATIC PAUSE: Feeling

What is happening for you in reading this? How does this pressure to always be doing show up in your life? What does your body know? Let it out with a sigh.

Our Screens Are Junk Food

Just as your body knows how to reach for whatever is closest when hunger mounts, so too does it claim recoup time with whatever it can get. When we are not making time to regularly escape laterally, our "slowing down" comes in the form of zoning out. We find ourselves scrolling more often than we would like. Our apps and devices become substitutes for the reflection and presence our body truly needs. Unpracticed at unplugging, plugging in has become our convenience food for slowing down.

I'm not antitechnology. If you truly enjoy social media, go right ahead. The question is, Is it choosing you, or are you choosing it? We'll explore this in more detail below. We know our screens are notoriously addictive. Research shows that the social interaction and approval we get virtually boosts the feel-good hormone dopamine. When we reach for our phones and are rewarded enough, a pattern develops. Our brains begin to associate our phones with pleasure even when that's not the experience we're having. Just like any addiction, we habitually grab our devices for a "hit" and then consume garbage that leaves us more anxious, more sped up, and more dissatisfied. The cycle continues.

Spending time in nature, reliving a pleasant memory, and expressing gratitude also release dopamine. Perhaps what our body really hungered for in the moment that we picked up the phone was a few minutes sitting in the sun, a glass of warm tea, a walk outside, a deep breath. The ache for this kind of support went unmet, so the body took what it could get. It's much easier (and we're trained) to try to "satisfy" ourselves with convenience. Over time though, we begin to feel the costs. When we only know this way of "unplugging," we find that after a stressful day, recharging means numbing out. We're no longer connected to our body or the things that most nourish us. We're exhausted all the time.

There are certainly things we can do to minimize our reliance on screens. We can turn them off, keep them out of our bedrooms, make the screens monotone so they don't look like candy, lock our phones for certain hours of the day, and so on, but if we don't address the fundamental need our dependence is trying to answer, we'll be white-knuckling it for a long time. The answer to convenience-rest is not villainizing our screens, it's making time to truly nourish ourselves with real connection.

Pleasure Lives Here

Remember back to a time when you felt fully alive. Be as specific as possible. This should be a time when you felt 100 percent yourself and connected to your environment. Maybe you were hiking in a beautiful place, connecting with friends, dancing, playing with a child, creating something. Can you remember how it felt to be doing this thing? If nothing is coming up, that's okay. When I work with clients who find it difficult to remember a time when they felt fully themselves, I often ask how they played as children. This can tell us a lot about how a body is designed to connect with satisfaction, joy, and pleasure.

When we engage in activities that truly fulfill us, we replenish our energy stores. Our imagination, creativity, and curiosity are stirred. Taking big bites of pleasure by spending a day or a few hours in a feel-good activity rewires us to remember the small pleasures that are available to us in each moment. The more we drop into what makes us feel good, the more we can recognize what supports that in our day-to-day. It's not so much that when we feel our energy lagging, we start coloring or the like; rather, by regularly being creative, we're better able to sense in our day when we've lost connection to ourselves. We feel the difference between the kind of support our creative practice offers versus the convenience options we've been defaulting to. In that moment of awareness, we can make a choice. We can ask ourselves, What is it I'm *really* craving? Maybe we can't pull out our pastels right then, but we could spend a few moments looking at the sky. We could escape laterally.

When we're more resourced, we're better able to discern what supports us and what does not. Over time, we move to protect our well-being. We stop checking email on the weekends. We actually take a nap. We pause before grabbing our phone. These choices are made possible through practice.

SOMATIC PRACTICE: Escaping Laterally

In my twenties, I interned at a national food magazine. I spent most of my time editing their recipe index, which involved doing a repetitive task in front of a screen over and over for several hours. I longed to be in the test kitchen or, even better, writing about real food, but my day-to-day couldn't have been further from that reality. One of the editors of the magazine prepared a cup of matcha every day at 3:00 p.m. One day, she popped over to my cubicle and invited me to join her. I'd never drunk matcha. I'd never spent time focusing on a cup of tea. There, in a sea of gray carpet and florescent lighting, amid the hum of keyboards clicking, we got quiet. After whisking the verdant powder, she handed me a delicate cup that gracefully fit in the palm of my hand. As the warm tea made its way through my body, I felt human again. Our conversation was sparse. We just sipped. I found that even in an environment as uninspiring and sterile as cubicle-ville, it was possible to find myself. I have much gratitude for this wise teacher and friend who showed me the way.

Now it's your turn. The somatic practice below I consider an embodied tea break.

Place yourself in a space that is free from screens. If you're able, I recommend doing this practice standing, although it can also be done sitting or moving just your head or eyes. Note, you can also listen to a guided audio version of this practice at http://www.newharbinger.com/50614.

Use five minutes to take a 360-degree turn in place in your environment. Don't worry about setting a timer; just make an intention. As you begin, allow yourself to take in where you are. Notice where your eyes are drawn. Notice what you enjoy or find beautiful (rather than things that need to be cleaned or fixed). Notice the colors and textures. Make incremental adjustments to take up the full five minutes turning in your space.

If you're seated, do this practice by adjusting your body in your chair. If you're moving from the head, turn your neck fully to one side and then slowly turn in the other direction. You can then turn around and do the same thing, taking in what was behind you.

As you scan your space, tune in to your other senses.

What is the most distant sound you can hear?

What is the closest sound?

What smells are present?

Is there anything on your tongue? Memories of your last meal?

Ask yourself: What does my body need right now? To stretch? To yawn? To breathe more deeply? To lie down?

Can you let yourself have that?

Take a moment to reflect on this experience. What did it show you?

Am I Choosing It, or Is It Choosing Me?

Just as we all have our favorite go-to junk foods, our bodies have their own go-to convenience ways they try to nourish themselves. Before we engage in these activities, we might ask, Am I choosing it, or is it choosing me? When we're making choices that support us, we feel expansive and empowered. We're able to actually enjoy what we're doing. There's nothing wrong with *choosing* to enjoy a pack of gummy worms, just like there's nothing wrong with *choosing* reality TV. On the other end of the spectrum, when it's choosing us, we often don't feel so amazing. We discover that:

- What we're doing makes us feel bad (not enough, jealous, angry, depressed)

- We've lost connection to what our body is feeling

- We get sucked in, despite our best intentions

- FOMO (fear of missing out) initiates our engagement

- We're losing sleep to do it

- We feel lost (we question what we're doing with our life)

- We prefer to do it in secret

- We feel discouraged about ourselves and our place in the world

- We feel possibilities diminish

JOURNAL: Aligning Body and Mind

Give yourself thirty minutes to an hour to reflect on the following questions. Don't overthink your answers; let whatever arises arise. If nothing comes to mind for a question, skip it and come back to it later. Let your answers come forward with more than words. Feel free to draw, doodle, color, move or do however else your body wants to express itself.

When it's choosing us, we're starved for another kind of nourishment. What are these convenience ways of "resting" for you? They may involve your smartphone or tablet, or people and projects that you don't truly enjoy. You may have also found you've tried to limit or quit these activities but it's difficult to do. When you find yourself engaged in these activities, you might ask, What am I *really* hungry for?

Reflect on the following prompt:

I spend more time than I would like doing... (list as many items as come to mind)

For each item on your list, ask:

1. Before I engage in this activity, I feel...

2. After I engage in this activity, (in general) I feel...

3. After I engage in this activity, my body feels...

If you're not able to answer these questions, let this reflection be a prompt to begin to notice what you're feeling after doing one of the activities on your list. This is not about being wrong or bad or deficient. The systems we live under drive us toward spending our time in ways that prioritize profiting from us rather than supporting us. Here, we're simply taking a moment to notice without judgment what's going on.

What Are You Craving?

Like taking time to drink a cup of tea, activities that nourish us help us feel more present. Here's what we may notice during and afterward:

- We feel energized.

- We're not compromising on sleep (the activity may even be sleep).

- We feel connected to a bigger perspective.

- We may feel calm.

- We feel gratitude and appreciation.

- We see solutions.

- We're present.

- Some part of us is relieved, pleased, or glad we took this time.

- We're better able to be with what is.

- We feel more "ourselves."

And here are some activities that may support us in feeling this way:

- Napping

- Drinking a glass of water

- Getting more sleep in general

- Going on a walk

- Spending time in the sun, rain, or shade

- Stargazing

- Sitting under a tree

- Meditating

- Coloring, painting, or other acts of creation

- Staring out a window

- Stretching

- Being with an animal

- Hiking

- Following your breath

- Taking in your environment using all five senses

JOURNAL: Aligning Body and Mind

Return to the list you made in the previous exercise. Reflect on the following:

- When I feel (insert item from your response to #2 in the journal prompt above), maybe my body needs...

- Here are some ways I might explore truly meeting that need...

SOMATIC PRACTICE: Try It On

You should now have a list of your convenience-rest go-tos and the nutritive rest your body is actually craving. Now the real work begins. Make a commitment to "try on" a new practice for a period.

- List your convenience-rest activities next to your nutritive-rest practices on a sheet of paper. Put this list somewhere you can see it.

- Which practice would you like to commit to? Rather than what you *should* do, what does your body want?

- How often would you like to do it? Choose a frequency that feels like a goal but is also accessible. Rather than every day, for example, maybe every other day or three times in the next week or whenever you notice your body reaching for convenience.

- Do you need to tell anyone to make this possible? Do you need to ask a friend or partner for gentle support?

- When will you check in with yourself to assess how it's going? Put a date on the calendar. At the end of the period you decide on, notice how it was doing this practice. Is anything different after prioritizing time to come back to yourself in this way?

Part of this practice is also preparing for what can arise, especially in bodies of color, when you allow yourself to slow down. Because the program requires marginalized bodies to put others first, you may feel conflicted when you step out of this dynamic. Feelings of guilt, shame, and secrecy are not uncommon. You might also feel indulgent, like you don't deserve to care for yourself in this way or that you're letting others down. This conditioning lives not just in our individual bodies, but also in our families and communities.

As you engage in the practice you've committed to, if you notice these uncomfortable feelings showing up, don't be alarmed. This is the work. Can you notice what other sensations are present alongside the discomfort? Maybe after a 3:00 p.m. nap, some shame is present. But what else are you sensing? Do you also feel calmer? More present? More rested? By taking in the totality of your experience, you get to decide what to prioritize. You can consciously choose to follow the parts of yourself that know you deserve this kind of care. Though it can be initially uncomfortable, doing something different supports a reframe for not just yourself but also those who are following your lead.

What Is the Speed of Capitalism?

If only it were so easy. If only we could will ourselves to give our bodies more rest. Don't get me wrong—having the above information will be helpful. It will support you in noticing and beginning to practice new patterns that will feed you. But decolonizing the body isn't about tasting reprieve every so often; it's about living from this place.

How do we take care in an environment that's constantly reflecting that we're not enough? If racial capitalism is a fast-moving train, Black and brown bodies are running outside of it trying to keep up. The belief is that if we "run fast enough," one day its magical doors will swing open, and it will be us settling into a cozy air-conditioned seat alongside the others who have "made it." Making it means having access to resources and nice things, no longer having to work so hard. We know some of the folks we'll be sitting next to were born on this train. We know some had rocket boosters and "connections" who helped them pry the doors open. At least though, we'll finally be inside. We'll finally be able to rest.

The alternative, not running, not working ourselves to the bone, seems untenable. If we stop, the train will surely run us over. If we're not dead, we'll be in the gutter, disposable, and impoverished. This threat is always at our heels, so we fight for enough money, enough social credibility, enough clout to get to "the better life" that must be on the other side. But by overworking our bodies to earn the life of leisure we long for, we're seeking protection from the system in the system itself. It was not designed for our thriving. It is built on injustice, exploitation, and extraction. We all live in it, but there is no succeeding on its terms.

I'm not denying that money can afford us ways to protect our bodies in a society that threatens and withholds these basic needs. Money is the currency we all use. Money can support healing. But determined to work our way toward a better life, we run ourselves over in pursuit. We put paper, imbued with meaning by bodies and systems that subjugated our ancestors, on our altar rather than seeing it for the tool that it truly is: a means not an end.

Myth of Colonization: If I Work Hard Enough, I'll "Make It"

We're told that the difference between us and those relaxing on the train living a life of comfort is that they've worked harder than us. Or, they are simply smarter. We're told we can get where they are if we break away from the pack, if we're truly special. "I believed in all of the stories of America. You know, I thought I could be the exceptional one," said activist Philip Agnew (Allison 2021). "And very quickly over those years, over those Obama years specifically, I think, for a lot of us, the veneer of what the US has told us we could be and what we could do snapped."

There is no getting on the train. Its doors never open. It's structurally designed to keep our bodies running. We see this in any number of statistics. The median wealth of Black households in the United States was $17,100 in 2016. The median wealth of white households? $171,000 (Kochhar and Cilluffo 2017). During the COVID pandemic, Black workers in the US were more likely to work essential jobs, forcing them to put their own health and that of their families at risk to earn a wage. Systemic racism structures our society, and though we know this, we keep running trying to close the gap. We keep fighting for a place on the train.

As the train hurtles down its track fueled by dirty energy, Black and brown bodies, no matter how strong, cannot keep up. Without assistance, no one can. How does a body trying to run the speed of racial capitalism feel? How do you know this in your own body? We might find we're no longer able to slow down. We might find our thoughts are always racing. We might find that even in our downtime, we're darting from one worry, one project, one plan to the next.

How do we meet the behemoth of racial capitalism, its urgency, and its don't-give-a-damn attitude toward the global majority's actual needs to survive? How does one small person, in a river of bodies racing alongside, push back against the current? How do we slow our swept-upedness enough to escape laterally? We see racial capitalism as the juvenile, inept system that it is, and we meet it with something older, wiser, and much more knowing. We meet it with ritual.

The Necessity of Ritual

It is in inviting ritual that we take the dollar off our proverbial altars and put something else, something truer, there instead. That something else is how we live from a place of nourishment and well-being rather than tasting it infrequently. It is how we can be in practices, like the one you committed to above, with regularity. In ritual, we meet our ancestors and guides, we feel the support of the knowing earth, we contact our own strength and resilience, and these entities hold us. Ritual connects us with an essential decolonizing truth: I have arrived.

Decolonizing Truth: I Have Arrived

Ritual is any practice that intentionally connects us with ourselves, our community, our ancestors, and a larger organizing principle or intelligence. You may call that organizing intelligence spirit, God, the Universe, or any other name that points to the unseen animating force that radiates aliveness. A ritual is a practice, something we do with frequency based on certain conditions, but not all practices are rituals. Though we may consider a certain set of routines our "ritual," this choreography is a practice until we invite intention and listen for this organizing intelligence in it. An evening routine, for example, becomes ritual when we take time to honor, offer, and reflect. There are personal, familial, and communal rituals that can happen anytime—daily, seasonally, at harvest time, during a life passage or threshold. A ritual can be as simple as lighting a candle for a loved one who has passed or as intricate as a multiday communal ceremony of dance, prayer, and contemplation.

Through ritual, we open ourselves toward the wealth of our present. There is nowhere to get to. We have arrived and are vessels for receiving. In ritual, we hear the whisperings of those who have come before. We feel their steady guidance, the medicine that is always available as we move through this relative world. We begin to turn toward it and trust it. This kind of sensitivity invites us to see more expansively. Like flowers fighting for artificial light and then moved into the warmth of the sun, the narrow pull of the train no longer commands us. We are guided by something much vaster. Writes author, teacher, and elder Malidoma Somé (1993): "Ritual is not compatible with the rapid rhythm that industrialism has injected into life. So whenever ritual happens in a place commanded by or dominated by a machine, ritual becomes a statement against the very rhythm that feeds the needs of that machine" (19).

Somé's use of the word "machine" I equate to my use of "the program." It is through ritual that we counter consumerism and exploitation with that which is generative, interdependent, and sustainable. By being in and practicing ritual, we cut through the hazy confusion of the colonialist-imperialist-white-supremacist-capitalist patriarchy. We hear, see, smell, taste, feel, and trust the life-giving, ancestral wisdoms that have lain dormant in our bones.

Moving from "on Time" to "in Time"

Ritual unfolds us to time in a different way.

What is an hour to a ribbon of smoking palo santo?

What is a day to the thumping drum?

What is tomorrow to a tumble of rose quartz?

What is a success to the great, greats of your name who came before?

What is power to our tender beating hearts?

This sensory knowing is three-dimensional and unbound by a conditioned sense of "making it." It is now.

Amber McZeal (2021), writer, vocalist, sacred scholar, and member of the Rooted Global Village, a virtual community building an "ecology of care" for communal healing and liberation, puts it this way: "The human mind tends to be pretty literal. Even though it can jump around, it doesn't necessarily have the access to different kinds of time. We can think about it and analyze it and make structures and architecture to hold the ideas of other kinds of time, but…just like you wouldn't use a certain kind of meter to measure electricity that doesn't measure electricity, it's like you need another kind of perspective to even understand or move within time."

That different perspective is ritual. Ritual moves us from trying to be "on time," the framework of the train, to being "in time." While "on time" is getting somewhere, moving toward progress, and gauging our actions by measurable metrics, "in time" is something else entirely. In time, we open to synchronicity, creativity, and the everyday magic of the mundane. In this space, we are not chained to the clock but rather sculptors who shape time through practice. This kind of practice gives us not only more agency over our days but also more sweetness and kindness. Prioritizing time "in time" means internally claiming that you are worthy of taking up time in this way.

Perhaps you've come in contact with one of these magic time-shapers? They appear to move at an unhurried pace. They seemingly have copious amounts of space for creative expression. There is a quality of ease about them. We may be envious of these people. We may think that they just have a skill that we don't. More likely, they arrived in this relationship with time through practice, through protecting space for rituals that put them in contact with themselves and something bigger day after day after day.

For Those in the In-between

Ritual is often connected to the lineage of our people (or adopted people). When our heritage has been erased or complicated by colonization, as it has for most bodies of color in the United States, ritual may feel hard to access. What is ritual for those who are a mix of lineages, ethnicities, and spiritual yearnings? What is it for those of unknown heritage who have ancestors who were also oppressors? What responsibilities do we carry?

Being an embodied representation of the diaspora with both West African and white ancestry, and not fully knowing the traditions of either, I feel these questions distinctly. You, like me, may be searching for a spiritual home where all your pieces are recognized. While we all need to belong, it is those who don't feel they have ever belonged who are most shaped by this bone-deep hunger. It drives us because some part of us knows what is missing. We sense how the nervous system eases when meaning-making happens communally. We sense that the human animal was designed to live in deep connection with others, the earth, and its inhabitants. We intuit that ritual practices can help us navigate this knowing. At the same time, committed to decolonizing, we don't want to appropriate another's culture or traditions to meet our needs. We also don't want to simply go through the motions of practices that don't feel aligned.

For bodies holding a multiplicity of ethnicities (which, let's face it, is many bodies of color in North America), there isn't just one set of culturally relevant ritual practices that accurately reflects us. We might step into rituals that some of our ancestors engaged in and feel that the other parts of ourselves are left behind. The hunger we feel for full welcoming can be met only one way, by turning more deeply within ourselves. This turning in is the path toward creating ritual practices that fully honor our complexity. Trusting ourselves to create meaningful rituals may feel overwhelming. It may feel like a disadvantage to those who can more clearly connect their ancestry with a spiritual tradition they resonate with. But ritual in its essence is designed to turn us toward connecting with and trusting what guides us beyond the visible world. Learning to connect to this vast knowing that lives within and all around is a primary reason we come to ritual. For suggestions on where to begin, see the online guide "Elements of Ritual," available at http://www.newharbinger.com/50614.

A NOTE FROM RITUAL HERSELF

Ritual would like you to know that cultivating a relationship with her is like breathing. Let it come in on its own and release when it's complete. You don't have to become a scholar on indigenous traditions. You don't have to be certified. You don't have to go back to your people's homeland. You don't have to study under a spiritual elder. You don't have to close yourself off from society for several years. These activities may be supportive, but they aren't *necessary*. Ritual says don't let your mind create barriers. Barriers are how you've been taught to constrict your breath. "Don't you go relying on externalized authority to find me," she says. That constriction around your neck is the program. It squeezes you from your knowing when it feels threatened. But you do know. You *do know*. You, in this very moment, as you are, are the authority. These riches can never be stolen. They flow like gold through your veins. They're scattered like pixie dust through each strand of hair, smooth fingernail, blinking lash, puckered nipple, withered knee, time-padded foot. You walk with radiance. Of course, the program wants to steal this from you and to make you disbelieve. Breathe in fully and let the barriers quake in the torrent of your exhale.

If your ancestors perpetuated harm, you can acknowledge their confusion. You can understand that like us, those who came before were trying to survive in broken systems. You also understand that their spirit was embodied in a relative world ripe with misinformation. It is my belief that when we pass from this dimension to the next, we have an opportunity to see the impact of our actions. We can hold in prayer that the harm our ancestors both received and enacted is reconciled and healed. It is not uncommon for those ancestors who perpetuated harm to show up as the most present spirit guides in our lives. This is their way of atoning for their debt. We also acknowledge that we are not beholden to all our ancestors. We get to choose who we cultivate relationships with and who we do not. If there is an ancestor in your lineage whom you don't feel comfortable making offerings to, you don't have to. That healing work could be held by another relative or communally in your family. This is especially important to acknowledge when we know we have ancestors who harmed many or who harmed us. We can set boundaries.

In arriving internally, we acknowledge the crossroads we abide in and allow the ancestors we call on to hold us in love. It may be that we don't know who those ancestors are. It may be that we feel that no one from our blood lineage will "get" us. But we can expand our view and trust that if we were to go back to the beginning of our shared Black mother, there would be beings in our line who would hold us with compassion. We all have ancestors who were "misfits" in their time. We have ancestors who were queer, who were "too Black" or "too light," "too femme" or "too manly," or just "too strange." Our relative-world bodies are received by these ancestors as complete, whole, welcome, and congruous. In ritual, we connect with our ancestors who are now beyond the confusion of our world. We hear their guidance. We see how the lineages we hold communicate with, inform, and tease each other. We feel the overlaps. We open to channeling the practices that are most needed and best suited for us in this time.

This journey puts us alongside so many other Black and brown bodies in the Western world who are similarly multistreamed. In turning inward, we turn toward each other and, in this way, accept the task of illuminating possibilities for communal belonging where all may feel their wholeness reflected. Our bodies become conduits and disseminators for the healing we *all* need.

Everyday Ritual

Many of us have been trained to relate to ritual as something that happens outside of ourselves. Perhaps you were raised inside a church where the only conduit to spiritual knowing was a high-ranking male body who would then disseminate this information to you. Being devout meant deferring your relationship to the spiritual world to someone with authority. It may not have occurred to you that you're capable of fostering this connection on your own. Where would you begin?

Others may have experienced the industrialization of ritual and seen it distorted and used as an arm of oppression. Writes elder Malidoma Somé (1993), "One can claim divine sponsorship to justify actions that have nothing to do with the divine. One has only to look at American televangelism for that." Perhaps the harm you've experienced or witnessed has led you to eschew ritual practices as indoctrination meant to subvert and control others. Sadly, wherever humans gather, when they aren't consciously aware of and addressing systems of oppression, they are recreating them. There is no neutral on this front. And, even in spaces that are dedicated to more liberated ways of relating and creating society, these dynamics still perpetuate themselves.

Whatever your past experiences or associations, my hope is that this work opens new possibilities for relating with ritual that put you in connection with the wisdom of your decolonized self. This kind of ritual is alive, organic, and continually informing itself. Even when we do not know the ritual practices that go back to our mother's mother's mother's mother, we all have this inheritance in our tissues.

In the wise and thoughtful book *Braiding Sweetgrass,* author Robin Wall Kimmerer (2015) writes of this kind of embodied knowing. While camping in the Adirondacks with her father as a child, she recalls watching him begin each day by facing the sun and offering the earth a pour of hot coffee. As the stream tipped forth, he called out, "Here's to the gods of Tahawus." Kimmerer explains Tahawus as the "Algonquin name for Mount Marcy, the highest peak in the Adirondacks." She and her siblings instinctively knew to stop and pay attention when the coffee pot left the stove. As an adult, Kimmerer later asked her father about the origins of his offering, "Where did this ceremony come from—did you learn it from your father, and he from his? Did it stretch all the way back to the time of the canoes?" she asks. He replies, "'No, I don't think so. It's just what we did. It seemed right.' That was all."

The everyday ritual you're invited to engage with through the duration of our journey together is this kind of ritual. One that feels right. In my own life, my morning ritual includes West African, Native American, Asian, and astrology practices. It also includes elements that I can't exactly place within a particular lineage but that feel good to me. Not pressuring myself to "get it right" and instead allowing myself to "feel it right" is the essence of decolonizing the body. In following feeling, we reclaim what we've been instructed not to trust or to hide.

PART II

Reclaim

Our layers hold time, environments, memories, pains, triumphs, stories, and struggles. Some of it is ours, some of it is ancestral, and some of it has been heaped on us by the systems we live in. Finding our way back to ourselves requires that we move like water. We follow the cracks and trust where we are pulled. Rather than rushing, we allow.

CHAPTER 3

Reclaiming Your Body

Embodiment is not a destination, it's a practice.

—Rev. angel Kyodo Williams

When we begin ritual practices that slow us down, there's more space for connecting to and noticing our bodies. Just as we smell the swirl of incense, feel the vibration of the drum, and hear our breath flow through our parted lips, we start to feel more of our embodied self. This "more" is not always welcome. Aches and pains that typically get ignored now take center stage. A hollow in our belly rattles our nerves. The soft folds of our stomach over our pants make us feel uncomfortable. Our noticings contribute to how we feel about who we are. Given the expectations put on our bodies by external and internal pressures, that "who" may feel deficient. We avoid feeling our bodies because what comes up when we do is painful. Or, unable to feel anything below the neck, we relate to our bodies as distant strangers.

At times it may feel like our bodies don't quite fit. They don't move how *we* move. They don't look how *we* look. It's as if we're buried in a suit of flesh that doesn't accurately reflect who we are. The real us is "healthier." The real us is less scattered and more grounded, less anxious and more confident. The *real* us is comfortable in her skin.

When we feel this way, the voice of the colonized self is often present. It says: *This body is not the truth. I will fix it. I will be more disciplined. I will say no. I will start running. I will watch less TV. I will wake up earlier. I will finally be my "best self."* When you catch your reflection, you take comfort by saying, "This body is temporary." Then you get to business making sure that's true. You sign up for the detoxes, buy the apps, follow the plans, cut the sugar, and maybe things feel better—for a bit. But just when you think that *maybe* you're doing it, there's that voice. It whispers in the wee hours of the morning, *Your body is bad, faulty, wrong, egregiously imperfect.* When you hear that voice, it grabs you by the throat and squeezes. You can't breathe. Your mind tries to push it away. It races with more things you could be, *should be* doing. You are defeated. You want to hide. You want to cry. You want out.

The program says, "You are the problem. You are the reason you don't like your body. You are the reason you're unhappy. You are the reason you're alone. You are the reason…"

"Just look," it says. "See all the people who are better than you? See how thick their hair is? See how confident they are? See all the amazing friends they have? See how beautiful and successful they are?"

When we reclaim our bodies, we look at this voice honestly and squarely. We get curious enough, brave enough to suss the cauldrons of oppression that birthed it, and then we step into practices that challenge its authority.

Our Bodies Remember

I like to imagine the body as rich and deep stratified earth. Our layers hold time, environments, memories, pains, triumphs, stories, and struggles. Some of them are ours, some of them are ancestral, and some of them have been heaped on us by the systems we live in. Finding our way back to ourselves requires that we move like water. We follow the cracks and trust where we are pulled. Rather than rushing, we allow. We let ourselves wind down, down, down to the place inside ourselves that can hold our complexity with compassionate stability.

The practice of somatics is about learning how to let all our pieces belong. We do this by beginning to be in relationship with sensation, the language of our body, and trusting and holding with inquiry what this avails. Naturally, this journey brings stuff up. Part of what we're encountering is the historical trauma that continues to shape how "enough" our bodies feel. We're confronting the impacts of the colonial narrative on ourselves and on our communities. Our bodies hold these messages from our own history and that of our ancestors.

(Note: The below list may arouse intense feelings. Please skip over it if recalling abuses perpetrated against Black and brown bodies is too triggering for your body in this moment.)

Our bodies remember...

- Fire in our hearts and a hollow in our bellies when our beauty was stolen and commodified

- Explosive rage as sweaty palms cupped our breasts, drool fell to our buttocks, and our natural bodies were proclaimed "invitations"

- Digging and chewing and burning and stuffing and praying for a miscarriage

- The heat of shame because of skin tone, body size, eye folds, hair texture, and nose shape

- The frozen of fear because of skin tone, body size, eye folds, hair texture, and nose shape

- Clenched fists and boiling skin from catching lingering eyes on nascent breasts

- The burning of skin creams, the press, and relaxer

- Holding in more, more, more to fit the expectation to be less, less, less.

We learn that the only relationship to have with our body is one in which it is under scrutiny. The urgency to fix, improve, better, straighten, lighten, and slimify goes back. Scrutinizing our bodies was the path not just to prove ourselves worthy but also to prove ourselves human. "Thing-ification was colonialities' first move," reminds writer and teacher Báyò Akómoláfé. In the eyes of the colonizer, Black and brown bodies are things to be subdued and used. We've been taught to see only what's "wrong" with our bodies because contorting ourselves to fit these demands has meant survival. "Fixing" our faulty bodies is the only relationship to have with them.

Our bodies remember Saartjie (Sara) Baartman, and how her divine South African body was seen as an amusement to her European captors. When Saartjie was tricked into domestic servitude, she became one of the first Black women to be sex-trafficked in the early 1800s. Across Europe, Saartjie was displayed naked and sold as a joyride to lascivious men. Even after her early death at the age of twenty-six, Saartjie was dismembered and displayed as an exhibit at the Musée de l'Homme (Museum of Man) in Paris. She was laid to rest only when President Nelson Mandela requested her remains be sent back home to Capetown in 1994.

Though we may not have been taught about Saartjie, her story lives in the collective unconscious. It is a layer underneath so many others that shape our relationship to our own bodies. These are the stories that wind their way to us when we engage in our own healing. Rather than looking away, we look more closely in. We ask: Where does Saartjie live inside of me? How have I learned that my body is a thing?

SOMATIC PAUSE: Feeling

Notice what is happening in your body from reading this passage. Are there memories or images present? What sensations are here? Invite breath. Feel for what is physically supporting you—your chair, your bed? Can you let yourself sink into that support? Take a breath and let it out with a long sigh. Repeat as many times as you need.

Myth of Colonization: My Body Is a Thing. I Am Not Fully Human

Racial capitalism relies on Black and brown bodies being deemed "things." Otherwise, how could they be worked, abused, trafficked, and violated with impunity? We see this in our history, and we see this in the unrealistic expectations we hold our bodies to.

Decolonizing Truth: My Body Is Whole, Wild, and Wise

Somatics gives us a path of practice for beginning to reclaim what was decapitated by colonialism. With intention, we can confront the harmful narratives that run through our head by beginning to relate to our bodies with care and appreciation. We start this work by feeling for our own layers, and by recalling what narratives have gotten into us and thus deserve to be plucked out.

JOURNAL: Aligning Body and Mind

Go gently with this next exercise. Give yourself forty-five minutes to an hour to reflect on the following questions. Don't overthink your answers; let whatever arises arise. If nothing comes to mind for a question, skip it and come back to it later. Let your answers come forward with more than words. Feel free to draw, doodle, color, move, or do as however else your body wants to express itself.

Can you recall when you first learned there was something wrong (or something very right) about your body? How old were you? What was the setting? Did you see this narrative modeled in your family? In your community? How did you feel when you learned this? How did you learn to protect your body?

What does the person you are today wish she could say to that younger self? How would she show up for her? How would she care for her? What words of comfort might she offer? What are you noticing in your body now from revisiting this time?

Now imagine yourself as older and wiser, your eighty-year-old self. Envision this future you. How does she dress? How does she move? What is her home like? How does she relate to her body? What would this older, wiser you say to the you that you are today? What would she want you to know about your body? Let this inner elder write a letter to you.

What if there were nothing to change about your body other than the lens through which you are looking at it?

For Your Altar

I recommend asking this older, wiser self to accompany you as we venture further in our work together. Consider adding to your altar something that reminds you that they've got your back. It could be the letter you just wrote to yourself. My future me grows flowers in her front yard for herself, the bees, and all who pass by. I add fresh flowers to my altar space and throughout my home every week. When I see their cheery heads, I feel taken care of.

Your Body, Your Teacher

How do we begin to trust the wholeness of our bodies? The first lesson of the body is: *I guide you through sensation.* The sensations we feel in our bodies can connect us to memories, feelings, and emotions. As we try to listen for sensations in our bodies (which we'll do in the next practice), it may not feel like anything is happening at all. Or it may feel like the body is overly verbose in some places and silent in others. Like learning any new language, it can be awkward at first, but the more we practice tuning in to the body, the more we're able to discern.

Inevitably when we begin to listen to our bodies, we might not like what we hear. It can feel like the body is a neglected child. It's been waiting for our attention, and when we finally direct our gaze, it wants to tell us EVERYTHING, to show us all the places that hurt. This flood of information is often a response to spending most of our time not listening to the body. We don't want to face the pains, old wounds, and insecurities our bodies hold, so we have learned how to turn bodily sensation down—way, way down—so we can't feel ourselves at all. Given the complexity of our world and all that we are trying to manage, this makes sense. Who has time to manage the body's messiness alongside the stressfulness of life? And yet, when we do the opposite of what we may be inclined to do and feel ourselves more completely, we're actually connecting with a resource that can help us more skillfully navigate our days.

In all somatic practices, I recommend moving "at the pace of the body," that is, letting the body decided how much to engage. Initially, reconnecting to the body and beginning to sense what it holds can feel like crossing a precarious suspension bridge in a windstorm over a vast and endless expanse. It's terrifying. What's happening in our body is a lot. We might step one tentative foot on the suspension bridge, feel the unfamiliar shakiness below our feet, and immediately pull back. It is 100 percent okay to pull back. In somatics, we often use the fancy word "titration." As in, it's important to *titrate* our experience. This essentially means we ease in, and we ease out. We enter the practice, and then when we sense we're at capacity (but not overflowing), we ease out and reground ourselves. We did this when we connected with our inner elder after exploring some of the embodied horrors of colonization. (I hope she's still here by the way.)

As you begin to dialogue with your body, the initial surge of information it presents evolves. New neural pathways in the brain develop to help bring your body along with you more of the time. When you are connected with what is happening below the neck, you're better able to notice when tension, stress, overwhelm, and anxiety arise and to attend to them in the moment. Rather than a backlog of information that comes flooding in, connecting to the body becomes like riding a familiar (if sometimes choppy) river.

The following practice is a gentle introduction to connecting with your body in this way. Take this practice at your own pace. If at any time you feel overwhelmed, ease out of the practice. Come back to it when you feel grounded.

ACKNOWLEDGING TRAUMA

To be human means we will experience discomfort. We will all face pain, disappointment, hurt, and heartbreak. Getting more comfortable with being uncomfortable is part of what we're up to in this human life. Often though, these experiences of discomfort get categorized as trauma. We use the term "trauma" colloquially to label events ranging from slightly awkward to life-threatening. It's important to note the difference between being uncomfortable and experiencing trauma. Although we all experience pains, we are not all equally impacted by trauma. Trauma is an intensified experience in which our fundamental needs were not meant. We all deserve to feel safe, to feel that we belong, and to feel that we have dignity. When one of these needs comes under threat, we instinctively mobilize to protect it. When this mobilization is not met with adequate space to process, reflect, and "complete" what has occurred, we experience trauma. The uncompleted event gets "stuck" in the body, and any situation that faintly reminds our body of the initial threat triggers an embodied fight, flight, freeze, appease, collapse, or disassociate response. When our body has stored a lot of trauma, it can feel like an inhospitable place to visit. The body becomes a location with lots of dark corners and painful memories. Disconnecting from the body is a wise way (maybe the only way) to manage our day-to-day. If you recognize your body as one that holds trauma, it's important to go slow in this work. It may be helpful to work one-on-one with a somatic practitioner. Although it may feel like you can't trust your body right now, with care, I believe the relationship can be rebuilt.

SOMATIC PRACTICE: Your Body Speaks

Find ten to twenty minutes when you won't be disturbed or distracted. You can engage in this practice as often as you like. You can also listen to a guided audio version of this practice at http://www.newharbinger.com/50614.

Gently place a hand on your lower abdomen just below your belly button. As your hand makes contact with this part of your body, notice if any judgments show up right away. If the voice of the colonized self is activated, remind yourself of where this voice may be coming from. Can you make a choice to not let it be the dominant voice you're listening to? Imagine putting it in the backseat. Call in your inner elder. What does she say? When you feel ready, continue.

Broaden your awareness not just to what is in your mind but also to what is happening with your senses. What do you feel on your skin? What sounds are present? What about smells? When your mind drifts, bring yourself back to what your senses are perceiving.

Continue to keep your hand on your belly and begin to notice what is happening *in* your body. Feel for sensation. Notice the pressure of your hand on your body. Feel the warmth of your body on your hand. What other internal sensations can you pick up? Your mind may try to "make sense" of what you're feeling by labeling sensations as emotions, such as happy, anxious, or sad. This often happens very quickly. Right now, try to simply stay with the sensations, the raw data.

It may be unfamiliar to sense your body in this way. Below is a list of sensations that you could be experiencing. This is certainly not an exhaustive list, but it is a good beginning. Take a moment to scan these words. Are any of these sensations present in your body right now? What would you add? Jot them down in your journal. You may want to make a copy of this list and post it somewhere you can refer to it when engaging in the practices to come.

Sensations Map

Still	Floaty	Active	Inert	Frequent
Grounded	Airy	Vibrating	Blocked	Cold
Spacious	Ungrounded	Tingling	Heavy	Hot
Soft	Dizzy	Electric	Drained	Sensitive
Settled	Fluttery	Clenched	Dull	Gentle
Relaxed	Empty	Flowing	Contracted	Sore
Full	Spacey	Jumpy	Frozen	Tender
Warm	Light	Shaky	Stiff	Releasing
Radiating	Wobbly	Shivery	Constricted	Streaming

Sensation is how our bodies communicate. Over time, through noticing sensation, we begin to see patterns. These patterns help us understand what the body is indicating. This kind of knowing happens with continual practice. We get there by holding with inquiry what our bodies are presenting without trying to fix or quiet them.

Close this practice by reflecting on how it was for you. You are meeting your body, maybe for the first time. What arose? Was it exciting? Overwhelming? Confusing? There's nothing to do but simply notice. Take note of what you're feeling from this exercise in your journal. As you deepen your somatic awareness, it can be encouraging to look back at where you began.

Interoceptive Lily Pads

The term for being able to notice sensation in your body is "interoception." Interoception is the ability to assess and define how you feel *internally*. Developing interoceptive awareness is a practice of dropping below the head and tuning in. In the beginning, it's helpful to have specific places to "check in" with your body. The following are some places to listen for sensation. I call them lily pads because in the swirling waters of bodily awareness, these are locations we can "land on" to get a sense of the environment we are in.

Brain: What is the speed of this moment? What is the speed of me?

Breath: Where and how am I breathing? What is the quality of my breath?

Skin: What temperature am I? Are different places in my body warmer or cooler?

Chest: What do I sense in my chest? Can I feel my heart beating?

Belly: What do I sense in my belly? Can I access my gut?

Bladder: How is my bladder right now? Do I have needs?

Bones: How are my bones? What feels strong? Does anything ache?

Overall: How am I? Are there places that feel tired or overworked? Are there places that feel still? What feels good right now? Does anything feel wrong?

We all have interoceptive awareness. Anyone who's ever had a "gut feeling," "felt something is off," or "just known" is accessing interoception. In those moments, we may not be able to specifically name how it is we know what we know. If we tune in to our lily pads, the delicate and tough sensors spread throughout our soma, we get a sense of where this knowing comes from. The program teaches us to distrust the knowing of our body. But this kind of knowing connects us to the more-than-human world. It is in our bodies that we feel for each other, our environment, and our energetic and spiritual intelligences. When our ancestors were colonized, their trust in what the body communicated was seen as proof of their inferiority. These ways of communing with spirit, land, and other beings were cut off to "civilize" and "modernize" them. Although our people were harmed for expressing this kind of intelligence, it did not die. It was passed down wordlessly, body to body. It lives on in us.

Today, letting ourselves *know* in this way can set off an internal alert system that warns that this kind of knowing is wrong, dubious, or "less than." Not only does this narrative show up in the colonized self, it's present in all structures created within the paradigms of "the program." In school we are taught to deny or tune out the perceptions of the body. We are made to sit under fluorescent lighting at uncomfortable desks for extended periods of time "learning." We are encouraged to ignore bodily needs to conform to the agenda of the day. We are praised for the development of our conceptual and analytical minds while our "other brains"—our heart, our gut, and our intuition—are rarely mentioned. To get by, we learn to ignore our interoceptive awareness. The more we feel, the harder it is to "excel." And yet, when we have access not just to the agility of our minds but also to the sensitivity and perception of our bodies, we are more authentically ourselves. Coming back to our body and reclaiming what was stolen from our ancestors means bringing this sensibility back online.

JOURNAL: Aligning Body and Mind

I could reference a study or quote here to appease the part of our brain that likes statements, such as the one above, to be "proven." But wouldn't that be too ironic? Instead, I'll leave space here for your body to decide. How does interoceptive awareness support you? Check in with your lily pads. What do you sense? What do you know?

SOMATIC PRACTICE: Awakening Interoceptive Awareness

The following is a visualization practice. I recommend giving yourself ten to fifteen minutes in a comfortable place where you won't be disturbed. Read over the practice first and then spend a few moments dropping yourself into the scenario. What do you notice at the level of sensation? What arises may be quite loud, or you may not feel anything at all. There's no right or wrong way to do this practice.

Imagine it's late September and you're walking in your neighborhood under a bright-blue sky. Though it's warm in the sun, you're noticing a new crispness in the air. As you walk, a red maple leaf falls in your path. You pick it up. It's the first sign of fall that you've seen this season.

Now ask yourself, from placing yourself in this scene, what's happening in your body?

What sensations are present? (Refer to the sensations map above.)

Check in with your interoceptive lily pads.

Now you might ask, How do I make sense of these sensations? This often happens without awareness. A quiver in our belly gets read as excitement. Heat across our face gets read as anger. Sometimes our read is correct, and sometimes it's not. In this practice, you're invited to pause before creating meaning. It's also okay to notice that you don't feel anything at all. That is also information.

Interoception teaches us that our bodies are always taking in stimuli and are always communicating with us. They are the truth that interrupts the narrative of the colonized self that's often playing in our minds and driving our actions without our awareness. If we're able to listen to the fullness of what our body is attuning to, we see our world and ourselves differently.

Let's try another hypothetical situation with a little more charge. Again, read over the scenario and then take a few moments to recreate it in your mind.

You decide to attend a new-to-you networking event to make friends and build industry connections. When you enter the gathering, you notice you're the only BIPOC body in the room. People are happily clustered in small groups chatting. It appears that they already know each other.

Imagine yourself in this situation. What sensations are present?

Notice your interoceptive lily pads.

How would you name what is arising?

What actions might you take to attend to these sensations?

This last question is important. Most of us are not taught how to notice and take care of the sensations in our bodies. They arise unnoticed, and we subconsciously act on them. When we're able to slow down and take care of what is happening in our body, we make choices that integrate our conceptual and embodied knowing. This means we're less reactive, more present, more kind, and often more spacious. We'll explore this more in the next chapter.

SOMATIC PRACTICE: Putting It All Together

Let's weave together working with sensation, interoception, and trusting ourselves as whole, wild, and wise. Remember, it's important to titrate in somatic practices. Trust when you are complete. Come back when you feel ready.

First, make a plan to meet your body. This doesn't have to be something you do every day. You determine the frequency. How often would you like to spend time building a loving relationship with your body? Make a commitment that feels like a gentle nudge but is also possible. To prepare, carve out ten to fifteen minutes when you won't be disturbed. You'll also need a mirror. A hand mirror is fine to begin.

Start standing in front of (or holding) a mirror with your eyes closed.

Breathe.

What sensations are present?

What is occurring in your interoceptive lily pads?

When you feel ready, open your eyes. Be close to the mirror, not so close that you're touching but close enough so that your face is all you see. Look only at your eyes. What do you see in them?

If it helps you to stay in the practice, play with opening and closing your eyes.

As you look at yourself, repeat the phrase, "I am complete just as I am. My body is the body I am meant to have. I am kind to my body." Modify this language so that it resonates for you.

Notice what is arising in your body.

Where does your body know these statements are true? Where does your body question whether they are true?

You are in conversation with your body.

Repeat the phrases six to nine times, noticing each time what sensations are present in your body. Again, play with opening and closing your eyes to support you in staying in the practice

This is plenty for one day.

Close the practice by thanking yourself for the work you are doing. Take some time to gather yourself before going back to your day. This may include journaling, moving your body, or simply resting.

Over time, you can build on this practice by gradually increasing what you see in the mirror. As you are ready, take a step back to take in your face, torso, upper and lower body, and so on, and repeat the phrase that feels right for you. When you're able to do this practice with your whole body, experiment with doing it clothed and unclothed. Again, this isn't about reaching a goal but rather about being with yourself as you are able, day by day. Allow yourself to increase and decrease what you're seeing in the mirror by internally reading what you have the capacity for. Remember, this is a practice of care.

It is by coming back to the body over and over again, feeling for sensation, and holding with curiosity and kindness what is revealed that we begin to develop a supportive relationship with the body—one that is not about trying to suppress what is running through us, but rather one that makes room for and trusts sensation. As we strengthen our ability to connect with ourselves in this way, we will find we're also able to connect with our world more deeply. This possibility reveals itself to us with consistent practice.

You could come back to the exercises here for a lifetime. Take your time, titrate your engagement, and see what unfolds. This nonlinear approach is how we begin to detach from holding our bodies as things to perfect and instead recognize them as the ever-present, ever-wise teachers they are. We'll build on this idea in the next chapter by exploring specifically how to embody our inherent confidence.

CHAPTER 4

Challenging Impostor Syndrome

Sometimes people try to destroy you, precisely because they recognize your power—not because they don't see it, but because they see it and they don't want it to exist.

—bell hooks

As we come closer to our bodies, we notice that how our bodies behave doesn't always align with how we wish they would. At times they quake when we want to be strong; they cower when we want to be brave. When called forward to take up a little more space in this world and to let our wisdom come forward, we doubt our capacities and question our contributions. If Viola Davis, Yaba Blay, and Sonia Sotomayor can admit to at times believing they were impostors, I don't believe anyone to be immune. Even former First Lady and best-selling author Michelle Obama admits that, to this day, despite all that she has accomplished, she at times doubts herself. "It doesn't go away, that feeling that you shouldn't take me that seriously," Obama shared with author Chimamanda Ngozi Adichie. "What do I know? I share that with you because we all have doubts in our abilities, about our power, and what that power is" (Hignett 2018).

Why is it that so many of us, despite our accomplishments, feel like we're faking it? Why are we convinced that if people *really* knew us, they'd think less of us? Why do we trust that others' wins are proof of their legitimacy, while our own are mere flukes?

Breaking Down Imposter Syndrome

The term "imposter syndrome" comes from the research of psychologists Pauline Rose Clance and Suzanne Imes, who coined the term "imposter phenomena" in 1978. What they found was that "despite outstanding academic and professional accomplishments, women who experience the imposter phenomenon persist in believing that they are really not bright and have fooled anyone who thinks otherwise. For example, students often fantasize that they were mistakenly admitted to graduate school because of an error by the admissions committee. Numerous women graduate students state that their high examination scores are due to luck, to misgrading, or to the faulty judgments of professors " (Clance and Imes 1978). When their research was published, it gained widespread attention, which persists to this day.

Countless books, trainings, workshops, podcasts, and courses are dedicated to helping women overcome this internalized sense of deficiency. The general tone is: fix your mindset, reclaim your confidence. Still, even with more awareness and myriad options for addressing perceived shortcomings, women continue to be plagued with chronic self-doubt. A simple Google search reveals thousands of articles citing stories from high-achieving women struggling to believe that they belong in the positions they're in. Advice for navigating this anxiety-inducing terrain ranges from "focusing on facts rather than feelings" to "reciting daily affirmations" to simply "fake it 'til you make it." There's a reason for these myriad approaches. In forty years, we still haven't found one that works. Perhaps this emphasis on "fixing" women underlies the real problem.

When Clance and Imes conducted their research, the impacts of systemic racism, classism, and patriarchy were not considered. "Many groups were excluded from the study, namely women of color and people of various income levels, genders, and professional backgrounds," note diversity, equity, and inclusion experts Ruchika Tulshyan and Jodi-Ann Burey. "Even as we know it today, imposter syndrome puts the blame on individuals, without accounting for the historical and cultural contexts that are foundational to how it manifests in both women of color and white women" (Tulshyan and Burey 2021). Essentially, we have pathologized women for expressing the real impacts of living inside the program. Our emphasis on training women to stop feeling like imposters in an inequitable environment is akin to teaching folks that the solution to carbon monoxide exposure is holding your breath rather than seeking the source. The internal doubt that many of us struggle with is not a personal failing, it's a societal one.

The Body You're Born In

Your confidence is shaped by how society treats the body you're born in. The difference between someone who feels deserving of their accomplishments and someone who continually doubts and questions them is simply who's been conditioned to see their body (and by extension, themselves) as an asset to society and who's been trained to believe they are deficient and burdensome. Writes author Sonya Renee Taylor (2018), "...our societies have defined what is considered a 'normal' body and have assigned greater value, resources, and opportunities to the bodies most closely aligned with those ideas of 'normal'" (22). This normal or default body is the body we most often see celebrated, praised, and affirmed. It is Eurocentric, masculine, able-bodied, thin, and heteronormative. Do a Google image search for "CEO," "doctor," or even "attractive," and the predominance of the pictures that pop up adhere to these requirements. The more your body differs from the "default body," the less important it is. You are expected to play a supporting role, propping up and protecting bodies of greater value. One need look no further than the history of Black and brown bodies in Hollywood to see this dynamic.

Consider for a moment, in your own life: Who elicits head nods of agreement when they speak up in meetings? When no one is in charge, who "takes one for the team" by being the first to step into that role? Who feels no qualms taking the space they need to be comfortable? Who steps to the side when passing on a busy sidewalk, and who assumes the right of way? What do you see in your workplace? Your community?

Now let's flip the script and imagine the other side of this coin. What might it be like to reside in a "default" body? Maybe you had a difficult childhood. Perhaps your family even struggled financially. Still, all around you, bodies that look like yours are revered. The prevalence of white bodies you see holding positions of power, starring in your favorite TV shows, plastered on sexy billboard ads, and so forth convey that your body, and by extension you, have value. All around, your environment is saying: you are important; your ideas matter; you can change the world. How long would it take until you firmly believed and accepted this as well? How long before you expected to be regarded in this way? If you aren't able to "fulfill your destiny" due to outside circumstances, who may be to blame? It may never occur to you to consider the experiences of bodies who don't look like yours. If a Black or brown body feels sidelined by your presence, that is completely due to their deficiency, not something you have done. You're a good person. Plus, you know what it's like to struggle. You weren't born with a silver spoon in your mouth. You've worked for everything you have.

SOMATIC PAUSE: Feeling

Notice what is arising for you. Check in with your lily pads. Invite breath. Consider: What is my experience of trying to prove myself? What is my experience of being regarded as a contributor?

The Carbon Monoxide We're All Breathing

Even though bodies of color are saddled with being born into nondefault bodies, we must remember that inside the program, no one really wins. Recall from chapter 1 ("How Are You?") that we're all on treadmills; we're all running. We're all trying to "prove" ourselves and get "somewhere." The question is, who is expected to "arrive," and who is not? Who is expected to be successful? While we all feel a pressure to "make it," who is encouraged to take risks to do so? Who is given permission to think outside the box, challenge authority, take the unconventional path, and dream big? Default bodies struggle with an internalized expectation that it is they who are meant to lead the masses. Some whither under this perceived pressure. Others reap success and fame.

When only some bodies are meant to win, the accomplishments of nondefault bodies get reaccredited, pushed aside, and ignored. When Nepalese climber Nirmal Purja, known as Nimsdai, summited the world's fourteen highest peaks in six months and six days in 2019, obliterating the previous record of eight years, he spoke to a modest gathering of press, "Now we have climbed [the] fourteen highest mountains in the world. Right? Let's be brutally honest, if this was done by some European or Western climber, the news would have been ten times bigger than this. Let's give the justice to the people who really deserve the justice" (Jones 2021).

The Next Myth of Colonization Is:
I Am an Imposter

Black and brown bodies experience imposter syndrome because we are treated as imposters. This myth may feel harsh when you read it outright. *Of course, I'm not an imposter,* you may think. *I know I'm just as smart as anyone else. I know I deserve to be recognized. I know I belong in the position I'm in.* But though some part of you may know these things, does your body? If the root of imposter syndrome is systemic oppression that privileges, affirms, and empowers white male bodies over everyone else, it must be addressed at a bodily level.

JOURNAL: Aligning Body and Mind

Give yourself thirty minutes to an hour to reflect on the following questions. Don't overthink your answers; let whatever arises arise. If nothing comes to mind for a question, skip it and come back to it later. Let your answers come forward with more than words. Feel free to draw, doodle, color, move, or do however else your body wants to express itself.

Do you feel anxious that others will think you're not doing enough?

Is your body weary from working all the time because you've raised the bar so high that even you can't reach it? Or conversely, have you given up on aiming high because you've convinced yourself you aren't good enough to try?

When asked to take a risk that aligns with something you care about, like telling someone how you really feel or sharing something you've created with a large audience, do you find yourself getting smaller? Do you avoid the opportunity by telling yourself, "The timing isn't right"?

Do moments of success feel like luck?

Do you find yourself seething when someone else takes credit for your work, but swallow your rage to be a "team player"?

Do you feel like you're always wearing a mask?

Do you wish you could take it off, but the mere idea feels terrifying and impossible?

In my own life, imposter syndrome has shown up in subtle ways. For example, some friends and I organized a regular wine-tasting gathering. We are a diverse group of Black and white, queer and straight, mostly female bodies. During one gathering, a friend invited her neighbor, a hetero white man, to join us. Though the setting was relaxed, I noticed something curious in my demeanor. As I shared the flavors I was tasting, I found my body more frequently glancing his way. There was a new uncertainty in my voice. "Pear? Grapefruit? White peach?" He smiled, and we kept going. To the outside observer, there was nothing unusual about this exchange, but my constant glancing and intonation were more than acts of trying to include him in the conversation. Though my mind was sure I had nothing to prove, my body was asking, "Do you agree? Am I right? Though I'm with a group of my friends and you're the new person here, do I belong?"

If you feel like an imposter, there's a reason why, and it's not due simply to faulty wiring that can be fixed with a mindset shift and daily mantras. Our bodies are sensitive gauges of the unacknowledged privilege that suffuses our lives and world. We've developed instinctual survival strategies to adapt to this toxicity. These strategies keep us safe but come at a cost. That cost is not believing in and embodying our full value.

SOMATIC PAUSE: Feeling

Let's pause here to notice what's stirring in your body. Check in with your interoceptive lily pads. If there are locations of tension, place a hand there as a way to acknowledge what's asking for attention. Notice as you do this if any memories or images are evoked. As we acknowledge and untangle from the conditioning of the program, it's common for sensations to arise. Don't worry if you can't make sense of what is coming up. The body implores us again and again to release ourselves from the pressure to "figure things out" and asks that we instead simply be and notice. It wants us to trust that the wisdom it is pointing us toward will be revealed in time.

SOMATIC PRACTICE: Resting in Enoughness

Give yourself ten to fifteen minutes for the following embodied practice. If you identify as someone who struggles with imposter syndrome, developing an internal sense of confidence may feel remote if not impossible. Perhaps you can't remember a time when you've ever felt that way. Resting in our enoughness, however, is not as far away as it may feel. It's right here, right now, all the time. In this exercise, we can practice.

Take a moment to scan your body from the tips of your toes all the way to the crown of your head.

We naturally tend to tune in to the parts of our body that feel unsettled or achy. In this moment, though, I'd like you to let those parts of your body be present but focus your attention instead on a place in your body that feels settled.

What place in your body is comfortable? Rested? Available? Calm? What part of you feels good?

Check in with your legs, your booty, your hands, your arms, your cheeks.

Notice if your mind begins to judge this part of your body or flash images of how it should change. In this exercise, we're not resting on the image of this part of our body but in the sensation of ease itself. If your mind is challenging this, notice and gently bring yourself back to feeling. If the mind is too distracting, consider a more neutral location, like the top of your head or the back of your neck.

What is it like to fully be with this part of yourself?

Can you reside in the enoughness that lives here?

Can this part of you take care of the places that feel unsure?

What is it like knowing you can access a feeling of enoughness, anytime?

Masks of Protection, Masks of Erasure

Sometimes when I imagine our ancestors, I see their bodies as, in the words of Fanon, "cosmic effluvia" (Fanon 1952). They are literal beams of light. Hands reach up toward the sky, and honeyed rays shoot from their fingertips. They are rich in land and spirit. Powerful. The day the colonizers came, when they looked upon our people, it was like staring into the sun. They were so bright. So alive. So gifted. It was painful. The presence of such brilliance was intolerable to these men. It scorched their skin and illuminated their wounds festering with hate, violence, and greed. Uncomprehending of such harmonious power, they attributed the radiance of our people to an evil force. They used violence to subdue, tame, and snuff out our brightness. But our people were smart. At night, they gathered colorful feathers and grasses. They weaved masks to cover the sunbeams that radiated from their fingers, toes, and teeth. They prayed over these masks. They supplicated the gods to protect not just their bodies but the bodies of their children and their children's children from these depraved men. Their prayers were answered.

When arranged carefully, the magic masks shielded onlookers from their most vibrant parts. They drew less attention. They became "useful" and "entertaining." The masks helped them survive. But they were so effective, they shielded the wearer herself from her own essence. Our ancestors took these masks off as soon as they could—allowed the full exhale of their radiance when dangerous eyes turned away. As the world was remade by the colonizers, the masks became more necessary. Our people wore them more frequently. They were passed down to their children and their children's children and eventually to us, who were never shown how to take them off. The masks began to grow into the soft flesh of our faces. We began to believe they were who we were. We became hidden unto ourselves. Our honeyed light as rich as ever, just under the surface, pooled unclaimed. Also unclaimed was our connection to inherent enoughness— a knowing so powerful that others created a false world with unnatural rules and hierarchies to keep us from it.

Though this is a story from my imagination, it's a narrative that speaks to how our bodies adapt to survive when under threat. In the introduction, I discussed somatic shape. You'll remember that it is made up of our go-to practices and ways of being for navigating life. If you learned, for example, that to be safe in your body meant shrinking your physical form, abdicating your power, and silencing your intuition, you might take on this shape anytime you felt the potential for harm. That harm could be either physical or psychological. If that harm was constant, say you lived in a place where bodies like yours were continually portrayed as suspect, deviant, untrustworthy, unintelligent, weak, unreasonable, volatile, and unreliable, then diminishing yourself might have been a shape you learned to rely on frequently. Your body discovered that by appearing unthreatening, you could not only survive but also receive a kind of conditional belonging among those in control. This conditional belonging helped you protect your family, your resources, and everything else that mattered most to you. Our bodies are so wise in helping us navigate adversity.

The challenge is, sometimes our bodies are too wise. At the mere threat of danger, say, a privileged body enters the room, they take the shape they've learned to stay protected. In this case, what our bodies do may counter how are minds are determined to show up. Such was the case for me while wine tasting. I see this also in clients who'd like to feel more confident in bringing their ideas forward at work or in taking other risks that would help them feel they have expressed themselves in an authentic way. When these openings appear, the mask of protection solidifies, and they find themselves not sounding how they *really* sound or discounting their ideas altogether. Often after one of these instances, they feel ashamed, embarrassed, and more deficient. The voice of the inner colonized self sounds something like, "Why can't I just get it together? What's wrong with me? I should have just gone for it. This is why no one respects me. Next time I'll be better." Or maybe we do go for it, and we allow ourselves to be seen and vulnerable. We say the thing. Later, when we reflect on what happened, even when others read our actions as brave, and even when there is no discernible fallout, we self-flagellate. "I'm a fool. Why did I do that? I've shown too much of myself. Why can't I keep my mouth shut?" There is a tension between what the body is responding to and the wishes of the mind. Trying to will ourselves out of conditioned responses to systemic and historical oppression is a game we will always lose. Instead, we must look even more closely at the mask we've learned to wear and explore how we wear it and what it does for us. When we see it clearly, we can then learn how to relate to this shaping in a way that *works with* rather than fights its presence.

SOMATIC PRACTICE: Feeling for Your Mask

For the following exercise, give yourself at least ten to fifteen minutes.

When have you felt like there was more of yourself that you wanted to bring forward, but weren't able to? Or when have you shown yourself and regretted it? For this exercise, choose a time that doesn't feel the most charged. On a scale of 1 to 10, work with a memory that's about a 5 or 6.

Replay the situation in your mind. Place yourself back there as though it is happening now. Spend a few moments recreating the scene. What sounds do you hear? Are there others nearby? What is the vibe in the room?

Now ask yourself, what is happening in your body *right now* as you recall this memory? Check in with your interoceptive lily pads. Are there places that feel more tense? Places that feel like they're holding? Are these sensations familiar?

When you feel like you have some sense of this shape, release your body. You can do this by physically shaking your body, looking around your room to reorient, or calling in the support of your inner elder.

Next take a moment to journal about this exercise.

JOURNAL: Aligning Body and Mind

Give yourself thirty minutes to an hour to reflect on the following questions. Don't overthink your answers; let whatever arises arise. If nothing comes to mind for a question, skip it and come back to it later. Let your answers come forward with more than words. Feel free to draw, doodle, color, move, or do however else your body wants to express itself.

How did your mask show up? Did you feel constriction in certain places? Did you lose access to feeling? Did you forget you have a body? How would you describe the sensations that arose? How would you describe your energy?

What does your body know about this shape? How far back does it go? What memories are present?

What gets covered over when your mask goes up?

What gets protected?

Our bodies have learned how to take care of us. By seeing this clearly, we're able to relate to our shaping in a different way. We can ask: How is this shaping protecting me? We can then evaluate our present environment and ask, is this the right protection for this moment?

Asking these questions gives us power. Pausing when we see we're in our mask and evaluating "Is this needed?" is an act of aligning our mind and body. We can choose how we are in our bodies. We can assess the environments we're in and shift in ways that give us access to more knowing, more compassion, and more confidence. We'll practice this in the "Centering" exercise below.

Just as the body knows how to amend itself to stay safe, it also knows how to put us back in touch with the fullness of who we are.

Decolonizing Truth: I Am Enough

You are inherently complete. You are inherently worthy. You are inherently lovable.

Even if the mind doesn't know this, even if reading these words incites feelings of uncertainty, even if you doubt these words are true for you, your body does know. In its fullest incarnation, your body is designed to put your mind back in contact with this truth. You can do this through practice.

SOMATIC PRACTICE: Centering

I learned the following practice during my study with Richard Strozzi Heckler while at the Strozzi Institute. With their permission, I'm excited to share it with you here. When I work with clients, I tell them that this is the foundational practice of our work. In centering, we're learning to extend into the full form of our body and to reclaim our worth, dignity, strength, and vulnerability. We're feeling for the brilliance that resides in each of us and that we can always contact just under our masks. In centering, we're noticing how our body shrinks when we feel like an imposter and, through our somas (our feelings, thoughts, emotions, and sensations), reclaiming the truth: that we are enough. Even if this truth isn't available to our mind, we can reclaim it in our body.

Center is both a state of being and a physical place in the body. When we are centered, we are less reactive and more present, less speedy and more grounded, less unaware and more connected. We practice centering when we are not under stress so that we can access it when pressure does arrive. We're establishing a new home base for ourselves.

The physical center of the body is roughly two to three inches below the navel. You'll remember placing a hand there in the last chapter. When we center, we're staying connected to and initiating action from this place.

You'll need thirty to forty-five minutes for this next practice. You can do it standing, seated, or lying down. I recommend trying it in all these positions. This would be an excellent practice to incorporate in your rituals. It may be helpful to make a recording of yourself reading it and then play it back to practice. You can also listen to a guided audio version of this practice at http://www.newharbinger.com/50614.

Start by Tuning In to Sensation

Notice what is without judgment.

Notice the quality of light.

Notice the sounds that are present.

Notice any smells.

What do you feel on your skin?

Now, turn your attention inward.

Feel for the temperature of your body.

Can you sense your heart beating?

Is there anything happening in your belly?

What is your pace?

What is your mood?

As you drop into your body, you may find that there are places you can't access. They may feel numb or frozen. Simply notice. There's nothing to fix or change.

Notice the quality of your breath. Again, the intention here is not to judge your breath but to notice how and where it is in your body. You may find that bringing your attention here makes it shift on its own.

If your mind is active and moving, that's okay. When you notice it has wandered, kindly bring your attention back to your body.

Feel for Your Center

Bring your attention to the center of your body.

Place a hand just below your navel.

Your center is this 360-degree bowl from front to back and side to side.

Feel for your center in your palm.

Though you may want to close your eyes, I suggest keeping them open. In this exercise, you're practicing connecting with your center while staying in touch with the world. You want to be able to feel more of your environment and more of yourself alive in it.

Center in the Four Dimensions

Now we will intentionally center in the four dimensions: length, width, depth, and purpose.

Length: Unconditional Dignity

Give more of yourself over to gravity. Feel your weight dropping down, down, down. If you're inside, drop down through the floor, through the foundation, all the way to the supports of the earth.

Imagine the soil holding you. At the same time as you are dropping down, feel yourself extending up toward the open sky. Feel this connection to the vastness overhead lifting you up through the crown of your head. Extend into your full verticality, accounting for the natural undulations of your spine. Reclaim your length. In your length, you reconnect with your inherent dignity. Feel that you are regal, like Queen Nefertiti sitting on her throne. In our length, we embody our unconditional dignity. We claim that we deserve respect and acknowledgment because we are beings on this earth.

Width: Unconditional Worth

Staying in contact with your length, now extend into your width. Imagine a scroll at your centerline. Unroll it all the way to its edges. Let yourself inhabit your full frame. You may even extend your arms and legs wide to take up more space. What is it like to stretch into your full wingspan? Let your body settle into a dimension of width that feels like the right amount for this moment. Feel for the width in your breath. In our width, we feel our inherent worth and value.

Depth: Unconditional Strength

The location of depth connects us with time. Feel for what is behind you. So much of our lives is focused on what is ahead. In this moment, place all your attention on what is behind. In the back body, we connect with the support of the teachers and guides who have helped us arrive in this very moment. We also feel for our resilience. We recognize all we have personally come through. In our back body, we lean back into the support of our ancestors. Maybe they are known to us, or maybe their names are lost. Still, we can feel them whispering in our ears, always available to support and guide us.

Now tune in to your front body. Notice the softness of your front body. Feel your chest, belly, and face. In our front body, we connect with the unknown future. There is an inherent vulnerability to the front body. We are the only animal that walks upright, exposing our vital organs to the world. There is intelligence in this vulnerability, a receptivity. In centering, we're practicing not having to lean into the front body to predict, control, or buffer what is next. Instead, we can allow the front body to be soft and open. Extending fully into the support of our history and into our curiosity in the emerging future, we land in the present moment. In our depth, we connect with our inherent strength.

Center in Purpose

Finally, place your attention on what is important to you in this moment. What matters? It may be something large or small. What is bringing you to this moment? What is bringing you to these pages? Drop this knowing into the bowl of your center. Let it shape you. How does this purpose connect you to your length, width, and depth? Make an intention to stay connected with your center as you move about your day. Come back to this practice often.

Authentic Confidence Is a Practice

For a long time, I believed that the bravado I read as confidence was a quality that one was simply born with. I envied those who seemed bestowed with its magic. What would it be like to be so unwaveringly self-assured? Would I ever coast through the world so smoothly? Share my ideas with complete belief in their greatness? Step into a room with full command? Move toward a goal with 100 percent trust in my abilities? I've since learned that this kind of confidence is not inborn but is also a product of conditioning. These confident beings' scripts may differ from my own, but they come with their own masks and challenges. Cultivating authentic confidence, the kind that allows for the fullest expression of our humanity and that sources our value from deep connection to the wisdom of our bodies, is a practice. Our indigenous ancestors had rituals, ceremonies, and community to put them in touch with this kind of confidence. For us, centering is one way, a new/old practice that can help us reconnect.

The more you practice centering, the more center becomes home base. You start to notice in your body when you have left center, when your mask has unconsciously gone up. You sense when your length has collapsed, your throat tightened, your shoulders narrowed. Through centering, you know how to reclaim these places. You drop your breath down into your belly, extend it across your chest, straighten your spine, and sit a little taller. In the moment, doing this may feel strange. It may contradict what you really want to do (hide or overcompensate) or how you internally feel (not enough). But opening to this awareness and taking the time to reestablish yourself is profound. It communicates something to ourselves and to those around us. In your body, you're saying, "My worth is internally sourced. It is my birthright to inhabit myself fully. I am enough." Even when the mind is filled with doubt, when you interrupt how imposter syndrome is enacted in your body, something new is possible. You're tilling the soil so that more of your wholeness can take root.

To ourselves and others, this kind of confidence may not look like what we're used to seeing. It also may not feel in our own bodies how we imagine a confident person feels. Rather than unwavering self-assuredness, it is spacious. It doesn't push through or tamp down feelings of doubt and uncertainty; it welcomes them as truth-bearers connected to the complexity of the society we live in and our own histories. This information weaves together with what we're noticing in our bodies and determines how we respond. We lean back into the support of what has come before; we root down into the holding of the earth; we extend out to fully inhabit ourselves; we extend up toward the guidance of the beyond. We are sturdy even when our hands shake. We are wise even when our voice quivers. We are connected to our value even when those around us do not understand. There is a bravery in holding ourselves in this way. We're countering the narrative of what confidence is *supposed to* look like in the spaces we operate in. We find ourselves allowing more risks that expand our sense of self in the world. This way of being opens possibilities for others to bring more of who they are into view.

When we make contact with authentic confidence, we stop self-flagellating in those instances that we don't feel "confident." Instead, we relate to our masks as well-worn safety shields in an unjust world. Because we do not live in an equitable society, we know we may still need them. But rather than unconscious automatic buffers, they are restored to their original use and deployed with awareness as needed. After we've had to put a mask on, we do as our ancestors did and let the full radiance of our exhale come forth. We center to reaffirm the parts of ourselves that were severed.

The Mind Follows the Body

Something miraculous happens when we relate to ourselves in this way. Over time, the head begins to trust the body. Our actions beget new insights. In chapter 3, we discussed how sensations are the root of our feelings. Our stomach drops, and we read that as fear. Our shoulders lift, and we read that as stress. Our bodies also work the other way. As Buddhist monk Thich Nhat Hanh is often quoted: "Sometimes your joy is the source of your smile, but sometimes your smile can be the source of your joy." We find that by letting ourselves stand a little taller, taking up the space we need to feel the expansion of our breath and dropping into the sturdiness of our legs as they carry us from errand to errand, we feel more of who we really are. We are less frenzied and more grounded. Less ruled by others' expectations and more checked in to our own needs. More of our authentic being comes forth. We radiate, I imagine, much like those who came long before.

PART III

Release

You come from a line of bodies who are of this place, who walked this earth, who planted and harvested, who birthed and celebrated, who lost and wept, who dreamed and prepared for you. You're layered with unexpected relationships, journeys across great distances, many places called home, and beings called family. This vibrant weave of time, place, and history makes you who you are.

CHAPTER 5

Smashing the Oreo

Freeing yourself was one thing, claiming ownership of that freed self was another.

—Toni Morrison, *Beloved*

For bodies of color, imposter syndrome extends beyond relationships with white bodies. For many of us, a more painful reality is feeling that we're not "enough" among those who share our race. In a society structured by clear racial delineation, when your racial identity is not obvious or your behavior doesn't fit the role others expect you to play, it can feel like you live in the in-between—a kind of nether region of full acceptance and belonging within the racial groups you identify with.

While this chapter mostly focuses on the experiences of multiracial Black and brown bodies, the experience of feeling "othered" by the race you identify with is not limited to those who straddle racial and cultural identities. Monoracial folks may also not "look" or "fit" the roles society has cast them in. You could be queer and not fully accepted by your racial group; you could have albinism; you could be a transracial adoptee; you might have grown up in a white community; you may frequently be assumed to be a race other than what you are; maybe you speak too white or don't speak Mandarin fluently enough; and so forth.

I'm including this focus because it opens up the conversation of how racial hierarchy and the values of whiteness can still function and oppress folks within global majority communities. Regardless of the racial makeup of the spaces we are in, unless we are intentionally working to face and dismantle patterns of white supremacy, these values will assert themselves in the ways we colorize, racialize, and other each other.

Where I'm Coming From

In my own life, as the biracial daughter of a Black father and a white mother growing up in a predominately white Mormon community, I can't count the number of times my white peers playfully called me an Oreo. I suspect part of the reason for its frequency was my own response. I would giggle alongside them, believing it was a term of endearment. My friends were saying I was like them, right? White on the inside? I pushed away the alternative—that what they really saw was that I was different from them, Black on the outside. Growing up in the in-between is confusing. You're fawned over for having "good hair," challenged for acting "too white," ridiculed for being a "half-breed," and celebrated for your "exotic genes." Anything you do that departs from the racial majority is chalked up to that other racial identity. When you excel, you're rewarded with fleeting moments of acceptance. When you stumble, that other part of you is to blame.

Myth of Colonization: I Don't Fit

You're not *this* enough, and you're *too* that. Take a moment to consider if any of the following are true for you.

Is the culture of your Black or brown racial identify foreign to you?

Does it feel like you don't deserve to claim your racial identity?

Is it difficult to connect to communities within your racial demographic?

Is your internal racial identity incongruent with how others racialize you?

Do the values of the cultures you inhabit clash with one another?

Were you sometimes praised for having "good" hair or light skin and other times diminished?

Did you learn early on how to speak the language of the white world?

All of these can be indicators of feeling like a racial imposter. Racial imposter syndrome is the experience of not feeling like you belong within the racial groups you identify with.

SOMATIC PAUSE: Feeling

Notice if there are memories present. Feel for the sensations in your lily pads. Center.

Assuming the Default

An impact of racial imposter syndrome is becoming overly identified with the ruling racial group. You'll remember that the program, which birthed the concept of a "white" race, exerts pressure on all bodies to adhere to its standards. Anchoring your identity in whiteness doesn't mean identifying primarily as white. It means hinging your belonging on *what* you're able to produce. Your value is determined by your job title and paycheck. In chapter 1, we explored the difference between a body that is *what* it does versus a body that is *how* it is. Racial imposter syndrome dislodges us from connecting with our how—the indigenous practices that live in our bodies. Our *how* includes learning to incorporate this wisdom into our daily lives. Without the grounding and assurance of our *how*, we remain firmly entrenched in the *what*.

In a society structured by racialized capitalism, there is an intelligence in assimilating to the values of whiteness. Adopting the norms and standards of the program offers a kind of conditional belonging. We get to be

91

seen as "go-getters" and "hard workers." We're also given resources (though not as much as default bodies are) that make us feel like we're on our way to being "successful." To survive, all bodies of color learn this dance. But while some bodies code-switch between this world and the world in which more of themselves can come forward, for bodies that feel like racial imposters, there's just one code: the white code. Living within the white code keeps you always striving for external approval of your enoughness. Rather than the balm of being in spaces where you are worthy simply for being who you are, your approval hinges on how you feed the system, aka what you produce. Over time, it's more comfortable to stay familiarly uncomfortable and entrenched in that world. Who are you otherwise?

When confronted with spaces in which your marginalized identity is predominant, such as all-Black spaces, there can be both an excitement and a desire to participate while at the same time a sense of unease and foreboding. Will you be accused of being performative? Not Black enough? Will you be Oreo'd again? This time, does your "whiteness" on the inside become a source of shame? This fear looms larger than being deemed an "imposter" by white bodies.

You're Not Alone

Multiracial people make up the fastest-growing demographic in the United States according to the 2020 Census. More than thirty-three million Americans, or roughly one in ten people, identify as being two or more races. Even with our burgeoning numbers, mixed folks often feel isolated in their experiences of being racialized. In fact, "multiracial people tend to face the highest levels of social exclusion compared to any other racial or ethnic group," says Dr. Sarah Gaither on the podcast *Code Switch* (Demby and Meraji 2017). We all have an innate need to belong. Part of belonging means we are surrounded by people who reflect our values and experiences. "We don't like ambiguous members of the group," she says. Historically and in the present day, appearance is the primary gatekeeper of belonging. If we can "pass," we get to claim that racial identity. If we don't, well then…

This isn't to boo-hoo that being light-skinned or racially ambiguous is more perilous than the violence exacted upon Black and brown bodies that experience congruence in how they personally identify and are externally racialized. Light-skin privilege exists. In a white supremacist society, the closer we come to whiteness, the more "valued" we are. The conversations we have about the realities of colorism among ourselves are necessary. At the same time, we must discuss all facets of colorism. A less-explored aspect is the way we ostracize and other each other for not being Black or brown enough. In addition to not being perceived as authentic, these slights come from not speaking the language enough, not knowing the cultural references enough, not knowing the history enough, and so on. Folks on the periphery may hold back from sharing experiences of feeling excluded for fear of being further diminished, side-eyed, or pushed aside. While it's natural for those with shared language and points of reference to share a bond, the ostracization of those who are less connected to these aspects shares a feature with white bias. Similar to the one-drop rule, which determined that any Black ancestry makes you Black, those who share our race but not the same life experiences become "white." We adhere to the tenet of whiteness that reduces the complexity of our identity to an either-or question: Are you, or aren't you?

We might ask, who benefits when our requirements for inclusion narrow? Colorism is a tool of segregation rooted in classism and slavery. It is designed to propel the myth of whiteness while forcing Black and brown bodies to push up against each other in its name. Belonging is determined by who comes closest to adhering to its values. But because whiteness itself is a fabrication with the sole purpose of dehumanizing others, it's impossible for any Black or brown body to become white enough. Heck, it's impossible for white bodies to be white enough (a conversation for another time). The mirage of whiteness requires an erasure of the self to come closer to its standards. We seek belonging by disconnecting from our bodies, the location of feeling, intuition, and our deeper knowing. Yet these are the very pathways that feed connection. The more we hunger to belong, the more we erase.

This pattern gets recreated in the other direction as well. To belong within a racialized minority, we shave off what we think is too white. We change our vernacular; we hold our bodies differently; we bring up cultural references that we think will resonate. Often this happens without conscious thought. Rather than a code switch, we step into the "role" of our ethnicity. But this "role" is a response to whiteness. Whiteness remains at the center. When we're the recipients or perpetuators of such behavior, we feel a sense of "off-ness" in our engagements. There's a film in our mouth.

The Tricky Third Space

What about seeking spaces for community that don't hinge on your racial identity, such as special interest or religious groups? For many of us, this is the majority of the collective groups we're in. It's wonderful to find a home in such spaces; however, unless these groups are also committed to unlearning structural white dominance, these patterns will continue to assert themselves. Race is always in the room. It's not uncommon for the burden of inclusion efforts to fall to the minority Black and brown bodies who are part of the collective. Let's face it, this isn't always work we want to do. But if this is a primary space of belonging, we take on this additional labor. Because these efforts tend to also center whiteness, there aren't opportunities (or enough safety) to question our own internalized white dominance. The work of coming back into relationship with our marginalized identities remains out of grasp.

You may also be magically uplifted by white folks as being the bridge to some kind of kumbaya moment between the races. This attitude is something like: "If more people were like you, this whole race thing would go away. We'd be one big mixed-race family." Your presence becomes proof we're on our way to a post-racial society. It also serves to bolster the confidence of the white folks who see your participation in the space as some indication of the hard work they've done to be antiracist. All of this ignores that racism is an institution. Burgeoning numbers of multiracial people will not pave the way to a post-racial America.

Smashing the Cookie

Smashing the cookie is obliterating the dualistic paradigm race is built on. It's smashing the *are you or aren't you* question to more freely inhabit who you are. I imagine these crumbs scattered across a kitchen floor and feel my body tingle with delight. It's messy, and like a Pollock painting, there's an aliveness in this masterpiece. We're told our identities are supposed to fit into predetermined categories. When they don't, we feel that we are the problem. When we smash the cookie, we release our bodies from the dis-comfort of trying to "fit" and allow ourselves all the space we need. We allow it to be messy, because it is messy. We direct our anger toward the forces that made our bodies wrong before we took our first breaths. We see squarely how we're *meant* to look, be, behave, sound, and act within the racial categories we belong to and feel the insanity of these requirements. A new space is created beyond the walls of expected conformity that allows for the truth of who we are. Like the beauty of scattered crumbs across a blank canvas, we are both unique and fundamentally the same.

Decolonizing Truth: I Belong

You are part of the human family. You come from a line of bodies who are of this place, who walked this earth, who planted and harvested, who birthed and celebrated, who lost and wept, who dreamed and prepared for you. You're layered with unexpected relationships, journeys across great distances, many places called home, and beings called family. This vibrant weave of time, place, and history makes you who you are. Like the ridges and valleys of your thumbprint, the terrain of your embodied memory, a memory both lived by you and shaped before you were formed, is singular.

Your originality makes you like every other human, past, present, and future, on the planet. We are all unique and, in this, exactly the same. Knowing this is where we contact what author Brené Brown calls "true belonging."

When we are oriented by true belonging, we risk reclaiming our most authentic selves—the parts of ourself who sings loudly to songs she's just made up; who doesn't try to hide her sadness and anger; who's tired of being productive, of trying to consume the "right" media, of working to know the correct cultural references, of working to speak in the perfect dialect, of fighting to have the right body size; who really only wants to wear comfortable shoes and pants with an elastic waist and eat almond croissants for breakfast with impunity. The more of ourselves we contact, the more we start to require no less for ourselves. Quenched by the secret internal spring of our inherent wholeness, we are willing to stand alone. This has a paradoxical effect. As we radiate more authenticity, more people are drawn to us. We find more real, nutritive connection. Lady Gaga took a risk when she wore her meat dress. Greta Thunberg took a risk when she gave her speech to the United Nations. What about in your own life? Doesn't it seem like the people who are the most audaciously themselves are the ones who find their people? They are beacons radiating what's true for all of us. As we feel for and unapologetically inhabit more of ourselves, we exhale. There is relief. We may also contact feelings of anger and grief. It's important to make space for these as well. Here's an exercise to guide your way.

JOURNAL: Aligning Body and Mind

The following exercise is an adaptation of a practice I learned through my study and teaching of InterPlay, an Oakland-based improvisational movement community that centers the wisdom of the body. Give yourself at least an hour to reflect on the following questions. Don't overthink your answers; let whatever arises arise. If nothing comes to mind for a question, skip it and come back to it later. Let your answers come forward with more than words.

Feel free to draw, doodle, color, move, or do however else your body wants to express itself.

Take a moment to write down all your intersections. Who are you? How do you identify? Include identities that feel contradictory or difficult to equally inhabit. For example, I am Latinx, I am biracial, I am white. Beyond race, how do you identify? How do you learn? What brings you pleasure? What brings you comfort?

Spend fifteen to twenty minutes writing, drawing, or moving. Consider using different colors or even pictures to represent your complexity. While this list may never fully be complete, finish when you feel satisfied.

Look over what you have created. What stands out? How does your body feel?

Now, choose an item from your list that you've felt challenged to fully embody. Make a list of how people who claim this identity are *supposed* to be. This should connect with how you've been pressured to conform. For example, *Black women are supposed to...*

Know how to braid hair.

Know how to cook greens and sweet potato pie.

Comfortably use the N-word like the women on Insecure.

Date strong Black men.

Don't edit yourself here; let it be wrong. Let be messy. Let it be what it is.

Choose another item on your list (this may be an aspect that is in conflict with the first item). Again, write how this identity is *supposed to be.* (Starting with two or three items is enough for this exercise. Eventually you may do this for everything you've listed.)

Now what do *you* know?

For each item make a list of what you know from your own experience.

I know as a Black woman that I...

Am not a monolith.

Don't know how to braid hair because it's not important to me.

Am not defined by my race and am also proud of my ancestry.

Don't use the N-word because saying it doesn't feel natural to me; there's nothing wrong with that.

Look over these lists and notice how you feel. What is it like to redefine yourself by your terms? What do you notice in your body from reading over the second list?

SOMATIC PRACTICE: A Breaking-Free Ritual

You're invited to symbolically represent breaking free of these constraints by smashing something. This is a practice I very much enjoy and has become a regular activity when I feel pressured to constrain myself or see narrow representations of identities I hold portrayed in the media. I recommend using organic material for this exercise. You're giving this burden over to a larger container that can take it and transform it into something generative. Some options to consider are rocks (if they break easily, all the better), lumps of charcoal, eggs, cookies (like Oreos), twigs (these you might break rather than smash), really anything that will feel satisfying to break and won't require cleanup. Glass, for example, is not a great option.

Do this ritual outside. You could be in the woods or near an ocean or lake. You can do this alone or with others.

Read your list of how you are *supposed to be* aloud. For each item on the list, break one of your items. I like to do this against a rock or other hard surface. You could also release them by throwing them into a large body of water. As you break the items, let any sounds that want to come forward have space. Yell, scream, grunt. You can also read your entire list and release the items at the end.

Consider (safely) burning the list when you've completed reading it. Watch the ashes burn in the wind.

Say, "I free myself from the untruths that demand this of me. I am a (name the identity). I belong within the human family." (Amend this language to make sense for you.)

When you feel complete, pause, feel what's happening in your body, and make space for what is coming up. Let yourself feel the support of the earth holding you.

Then read the list of what you know about your identities. Ask the earth for a reminder to help you remember what is *actually* true. See what comes to you. It could be a rock, a leaf, a feather, a picture you take of the sky. Place this reminder on your altar or other place where you can look at it frequently.

Unearthing Your Indigeneity

It's incredibly enriching to learn about the rituals and practices of your ancestors before they were colonized. Even if that information is unknown or inaccessible to you, exploring the traditions of lands where you think your people came from or where you feel personally pulled can also be a source of grounding. What were the foods they ate? What did they call the stars, moon, and wind? How did they move their bodies in ceremony?

As you engage in this learning, be careful to notice if the motivation for your research shifts from enjoyment to a hope that it will make you "enough." You know that's happening when there's a desire to "arrive," when there's an if-then equation rolling around in your mind: *If I was fluent... If I was initiated... If I knew the steps...*

Coming to this learning through the body helps us interrupt this pressure. Feel for where you're naturally drawn. Where is there curiosity? Where is there excitement? What would feel enlivening simply by being in the process? What is your body longing for? Time for stillness and quiet? Music and movement? Gardening? Food? Feeling new words rolling in the mouth? Rather than picking up a history book, this is about literally getting these practices into your body and reawakening what is already there. Coming from a place of care and pleasure pulls you away from focusing on ways you have felt shamed for not being enough. I see this a lot around knowing the current spoken language of your culture. For example, maybe you're Latinx but don't speak fluent Spanish. Perhaps some part of you really wants to learn, but this practice pulls you into if-then thinking: *Once my Spanish is better, people will see that I really am half Argentinian.* When you check in with your body, you notice your chest tightens and your throat closes when you think about taking Spanish classes. I'd like you to trust those sensations. This isn't the practice to begin with in forming *your* own relationship with your ancestry. It isn't kind. It isn't enlivening. It's rooted in trying to "fix" yourself so you "fit." Furthermore, you know that the Spanish were also colonizers. Authentic unearthing is different; it is about coming closer (as much as you can) to the parts of yourself that carry the memory of your indigeneity.

SOMATIC PRACTICE: Movement Mediation

Here's a simple practice for coming back into contact with the lineage of your people. I do this practice daily as a part of my morning ritual after sitting at my altar.

You can find a playlist of songs I enjoy moving to at http://www.newharbinger.com/50614.

Make it a regular practice to move to a song or two in the mornings or evenings.

Remember, this isn't a dancing practice so much as a *moving* practice. If you have background as a dancer, you may feel an urge to perform. This is not that. This is for you and your body. Notice if that urge arises and come back to your breath.

In movement meditation, the focus of your meditation is your body. Ask yourself, *What does my body want right now?* Can I let myself have that?

It may be that your body wants to move and shake vigorously. Or it may be that it wants to lie on the floor and let the sounds wash over itself.

There's no right or wrong way to engage in movement meditation. What matters is that it feels nourishing to you.

Over time, this movement enters us deeply. We find ourselves listening to ourselves in a different way. We remember to let ourselves "have" more of ourselves more frequently.

There's alchemy in learning to hold our many facets. Including more of ourselves from a place of openhearted inquiry awakens unexpected overlaps. We see that our ancestors, though from disparate places, were oriented around similar values. Our people lived sustainably with the earth and its inhabitants, marked the seasons and harvests with ritual, and prioritized community and family. Our individual bodies become portals for contacting these multilayered histories. Like colorful patchwork quilts, this tapestry of old practices finds new life and relevance by coming together through us.

CHAPTER 6

Tending Your River

Boundaries give us the space to do the work of loving ourselves. They might be, actually, the first and fundamental expression of self-love. They also give us the space to love and witness others as they are, even those that have hurt us.

—Prentis Hemphill

In front of you is a woman dressed in flowing yellow silk. Filaments of gold weave and shine through her black curls. She sashays past you, and you catch her scent, honey and cinnamon. Her brown skin glistens with vitality, and gold rings adorn her wrists, neck, and fingers. Realizing she's being watched, she spins toward you. A peacock fan flutters across her face. She offers a coquettish smile, turns, and continues on her way. Who is this confident goddess, you wonder? You'd like to know her. You'd like to *be* her. You have just met Oshun.

Oshun is an Orisha, one of the seven African powers found in the Yoruba religion, an indigenous tradition throughout West Africa and the African diaspora. Oshun represents all that makes life worth living. She is love, the divine feminine, sensuality, beauty, fresh water, and generosity. Oshun knows her worth. In fact, it is because she is unquestionably connected to her value that any of us is here at all. Oshun can be called on for many things. We can supplicate her to bring us love, prosperity, and fertility. She can heal the infirm and care for the orphaned. Any area of our life that requires more sweetness and beauty is the domain of Oshun.

I asked her to these pages with an unusual request. What can the goddess of love and abundance teach us about boundaries? Might she be able to show us how to truly care for ourselves while caring for and meeting the needs of many others? Likely, some of us have heard and used the phrase "making a boundary," but how might Oshun's gentle hand guide us toward where pleasure lives in this process—both as a giver and receiver of such requests? What is the role of the heart? Who better than Oshun, the Orisha who is the most generous with her love and the most able to take space (when not properly acknowledged), to show us the way? Let us begin by getting to know her a bit better.

A Yoruba Creation Story

In the beginning, Olodumare, the most high, sent seventeen Orishas to create the earth. When they arrived to the planet, Oshun, the youngest and only female in the group, was immediately discounted by the other Orisha. "What do you have to offer?" they questioned. "You aren't as strong and mighty as we are. You can't make thunder or build the sky. We don't need you. We'll make the world on our own."

This was the ultimate insult for Oshun. How could they not see her power? Rather than arguing, she simply replied, "Okay, let's see how you do." She left the earth and sat on the moon "powdering her face," as storyteller and Orisha high priestess, Luisah Teish tells it (EMAVoicesOfTheEarth 2012).

When Oshun left the earth, all the sweet water vanished. The rivers and waterfalls no longer flowed. The lakes dried and cracked. In a world without fresh water, the other Orisha were impotent. Ogun couldn't forge iron. Obatala couldn't shape the children. Chango couldn't make fire.

The Orisha returned to Olodumare and said, "The task you've given us is impossible. There's no sweet water." Olodumare looked at the group of Orisha before her and asked, "Hmmm…but one of you is missing. Where is Oshun?" "Oh, her?" they asked puzzled. "She's of no use. We sent her away." Olodumare replied, "Ah, but you have no idea who Oshun is. Without her, *you* are of no use." Olodumare sent for Oshun and instructed the other Orishas that their first job in creating the world was to apologize to her. The Orisha acknowledged their mistake and humbly asked Oshun for her forgiveness. She accepted and agreed to return with them to the earth, but not before reminding them to *never* misjudge her again.

Feeling her worth properly acknowledged, the sweet waters once again began to flow. The earth was suffused with love, beauty, generosity, kindness, and connection. The Orishas could move forward with their work.

The Brilliance and Distortion of Oshun

Oshun is the Orisha of life. Teish reminds us of her power and poetry: "Oshun is the unbridled eroticism of nature. She is the power of attraction that causes a particle and a wave to interact with each other. She is why atoms and molecules hold together. She is why plants entwine their roots and animals make mating calls to each other. Let's not get it confused. The sweet moisture of the earth is the essence of Oshun. Nothing can be done on this planet without her" (EMAVoicesOfTheEarth 2012).

Oshun is our reminder that there is no life without the divine feminine. There is no life without water. She runs through all that senses and breathes. Because she is in all living things, Oshun is in you. In the body, Oshun is the surge of the erotic. She is the spark of creativity and the blush of a first kiss. She is a day tangled in the sheets with our lover and the magnificent sunrise sky that catches our breath in surprise. She is our yearning for a kind shoulder to rest our head upon and our craving to be enraptured by the slow and sultry. Oshun is our heart overflowing with appreciation for the hands that made us soup and our breasts overflowing with milk to nourish a hungry babe until contented. Oshun is not interested in winning or conquering. She's here to inspire, love, and seduce. When we're riding the wisdom of Oshun, praise, acknowledgment, and affirmation become our manna.

And yet, as illustrated in the above story, Oshun's power is often underestimated and diminished. In our world, rather than seeing the erotic as fuel and vulnerability as power, forces intimidated by the expansiveness of this intelligence transfigure it into weakness. Today we see how the program has distorted and commercialized the brilliance of Oshun. If we dream for a world where all can thrive, we are naive. If we freely express our sexuality, we are to blame for whatever may come our way. "In order to perpetuate itself, every oppression must corrupt or distort those various sources of power within the culture of the oppressed that can provide energy for change," writes Audre Lorde (2007) in her essay "Uses of the Erotic." "For women, this has meant a suppression of the erotic as a considered source of power and information within our lives" (30). We learn that what the heart longs for is shameful and a weakness.

Myth of Colonization: My Vulnerability Is Weakness

The heart connects us with our vulnerability. It is the location where we feel our needs for intimacy, connection, and belonging. Societally, this kind of openness is often regarded as a kind of weakness. We are shown that when we are vulnerable, we make ourselves open for attack. If we reach out for connection and are wounded, we are at fault. We made ourselves "too vulnerable." But there is another truth as well: vulnerability is a requirement for life. From the flower with petals curled back to the frog's full-throated mating call, the world is created through longing. The heart is where we feel the surge of all that supports existence. Rather than seeing these pulsings as indications of power, the program has taught us to regard them as shameful needs that will invariably one day lead to our ruin. The intelligence of Oshun, the erotic that runs in and through us, becomes a mark of inferiority. Our fears of potentially being wounded from sharing our vulnerability are not unfounded. We can likely think of many examples from our own lives where this has happened.

Similarly on the national stage, the closer the discourse comes to matters of the heart, the more likely it is discounted. I'm reminded of

Marianne Williamson's 2020 presidential bid. Williamson ran a humanist-centered campaign and spoke of "initiating a season of moral repair" and making "humanity itself America's greatest ally." She advocated for a holistic educational system similar to Canada's, sensible animal-welfare standards, urgent commitments to the environment, the creation of a cabinet-level Department of Children and Youth to reduce America's infant mortality rates—positions that I imagine would please the goddess. Her presence on the political stage was widely ridiculed. Rumors raged that painted her as remarkably unqualified and kooky. Her former position as a spiritual advisor to Oprah was played up while her history running a successful nonprofit delivering food to AIDS patients in the 1980s was played down. And yes, Williamson was unique, she spoke of an American revolution fueled by the power of love, but regardless of your politics, did the best-selling author belong on that stage any less than Andrew Yang, a businessman; Pete Buttigieg, a mayor of a tiny town; or Donald Trump, a wealthy heir and reality star?

An environment that belittles Oshun becomes a desert of what sustains life. Today we see this quite literally on a global scale. From lack of care, the water sources we rely on are becoming polluted and drying up. The planet continues to warm. Species are dying. Our own extinction is on the horizon. In our own lives, the kind of intimacy that engenders belonging can also provoke internal tension. We long for a sense of community and to feel less alone, but unpracticed at this way of relating (and taught to fear our own vulnerability), we are both attracted to and terrified of the prospect of being seen for who we really are. All of this plays out distinctly in relationship to our boundaries.

Oshun and Boundaries

Vulnerability is a requirement for intimacy. It is how we invite true union. It is also a requirement for connecting to the vibrancy of the erotic that pulses through us. Without this foundation, our relationship to Oshun is confused. This confusion shows up in our boundaries. You may feel like you just can't do boundaries. Or you may wish you did them a little less stringently. Relationships are draining and complicated. You're at the whim of a familiar inner push and pull. You push toward connection and then shrink back when it becomes too much. Your boundaries become a kind of shield that you enforce as a defense or, sometimes, as a weapon.

It's important to have a lot of compassion for the part of us that struggles with intimacy. We might ask: What models did I have? What does my family do? What do I see in my community and the larger world? How are women who look like me supposed to behave? We are products of the environments we grow up in. More on this in a bit.

I've invited Oshun to this exploration of boundaries because she reminds us of their true intention. Boundaries can actually help us stay *in* relationship. They are a dance that centers our ability to care and love ourselves and others. "Boundaries are the distance at which I can love you and me simultaneously," reminds somatics practitioner and author Prentis Hemphill (Brown 2021, 129). They are needed to prioritize all parties' well-being. When we make a boundary, we're asking: What is the space needed to stay in connection to my heart? What is the space needed to also care for you? I'm not just caring for you, and I'm not just caring for myself; I'm dancing with holding us both.

When Oshun went to sit on the moon, she took that far-off distance because it was the only way to stay connected to love—love for herself and enough love for the world that she could come back. Sometimes it can feel like we need that much space (especially when another is causing harm). Taking a lot of space is okay. But our boundaries are not a defense to shut down connection; they are what supports us to stay in relationship and still connected to love. How do we do that? How do we rewrite our relationship to boundaries as something we enact from a place of care? To explore that, let's first take a closer look at how you may be doing them now.

Overly Porous and Overly Firm

Some of us have boundaries that are overly porous. We let in too much. We give too much. We don't know where we end and another begins. And some of us have boundaries that are too firm. Nothing gets in and nothing gets out. We feel untrusting of our world and isolate ourselves from it.

How we learn to do our boundaries happens in a social context. We're shaped by what we see happening in our families, our communities, and the larger world. Systemic oppression impacts our relationship to our boundaries. If, for example, it's been shown to us that we can't have agency over certain aspects of our lives, that we're meant to always be taking care of others, this impacts what boundaries we think are available to us. This also happens at a community level. If the community I live in is suddenly split by a six-lane highway that nobody voted for, this impacts the boundaries I believe I'm allowed to have. Experiences of trauma also impact our boundaries. If we have been hurt by those we trust, we may learn that letting our walls down is fundamentally unsafe. We hold in what could create connection because history has shown us that not doing so will cause harm to ourselves and others.

Here's a closer look at how this may show up in our lives:

When we're overly porous, we...	When we're overly walled, we...
Find it extremely uncomfortable to express our needs	Rarely express our emotions (even with those we are closest to)
Find ourselves often in the role of the listener	Choose unavailable partners
Find ourselves often in the role of the caretaker	Hate talking about our "feelings"
May find that we have a lot of drama in our lives due to the relationships we're in	Like to keep the past in the past

When we're overly porous, we...	When we're overly walled, we...
Find it hard to make decisions (because we're focused on the needs of others)	Keep our shit together at all costs: "Never let them see you sweat"
Worry about letting people down	Default to not talking about things that bother us
Say yes more often than we would like because we're driven by guilt and anxiety	Prefer to keep areas of our life completely separated
Fear being rejected	Cut people loose when they get too close

SOMATIC PAUSE: Feeling

What do you know about how you do boundaries? How do boundaries feel in your body? You may think of a situation where you had to make a boundary or wanted to make a boundary. Notice what is happening in your lily pads. Center.

A Journey with Oshun

Before we explore how we may unwind from our patterns, Oshun would like us to take a journey with her. Join her as she sits along the banks of the Nile, the longest river in the world and a magnificent expression of her power. Feel the depth of its intelligence—an intelligence that has sustained life since antiquity. Oshun would like you to know that this vast river pales alongside the powerful river of the divine feminine, the river of life, that flows through you. She's brought you here because perhaps in seeing the Nile, you'll understand a bit more about what is possible for you.

Oshun takes your hand, and with her, you float up. You're high in the sky and able to see the full expanse of the river. You see the tributaries that flow into it and the life that springs from it. You feel where its pace quickens and tumbles and where it is smooth and kind. From this vantage, you see that the river is a green snake cutting and winding through a blonde desert that extends as far as you can see. With your hand in Oshun's, you experience this expanse of water as she does. Even though you are far above it, you see net after net cast from fishermen. You feel the fish and the quickening of their hearts as they dart in and out of shadow. You sense the wind that moves through feathers of birds that swoop and dive from its waters, and you feel the gentle swish of webbed feet paddling below as hundreds of grebes float on its gentle surface. There are the calls of humans boating and farming and walking alongside it, and the cascading of water dripping down the broad face of so many hippos. You sense the crocodiles and snakes, the turtles, and the hum of grasshoppers. The urgent hadeda ibis sings: "This is you. You are of this."

Oshun tilts her head back, and with that shows you all the beings from the beginning of time who have been fed by just this one river—just this one expression of her. You see its rhythm, how there are regular seasons of flood and times of wane, and this is a kind of heartbeat. You see how this heartbeat pulses in and out but is always moving the river forward. The river is always moving toward its own yearning to expand into a greater vastness. On its journey, it feeds so many others. But for what it offers, it also receives. It knows the patterns of things. It knows birth and death, care and love, creativity and stillness. It brings this knowing everywhere it flows. This, you recognize, is real power. The power to shape life. When it finally meets the Mediterranean Sea and its waters mingle with those, there is a kind of celebration. An exhale. This too is the erotic.

Decolonizing Truth: My Yearnings Are My Power

In the practice of somatics, there is a saying, "Life moves toward life." How I interpret this is, what supports life within you recognizes and naturally flows toward what affirms it. Imagine this life moving like a river. It draws you toward what supports your thriving, if you trust it. It communicates with you through your heart, through your longings. As you follow it, you are strengthened. What your heart longs for only you know. It could be creation that inspires. It could be love itself. Some part of you—even if it is buried under layers of uncertainty—holds curiosity around a possibility. It may be inconvenient. It may be scary. It may be impractical, and yet, that surge of *what if* fills you with energy. Allowing yourself to be oriented by the power of your yearnings, you are pulled toward a richer life. Like the Nile, you wind and curl toward some unknown expansion, and along the way, you become an ecosystem, naturally offering and receiving with the many you encounter.

JOURNAL: Aligning Body and Mind

Give yourself fifteen to thirty minutes to reflect on the following questions. Let your answers come forward with more than words. Feel free to draw, doodle, color, or do however else your body wants to express itself.

Take a moment and feel your own heart. You may place a hand there if you like. Feel its warmth, feel its beating. Then ask it the following questions:

What does my heart know?

What does my heart know that I don't allow it to know?

What's at play in keeping this information subdued?

Imagine a River

I'd like you to imagine what would happen if your river did not have banks. Without a boundary, your waters would spill out across the plain. All that is around becomes saturated and drunk with your continual offering. The earth is soggy. On their journey toward the sun, waterlogged plants bend back on themselves. They can't support themselves. The river itself is directionless. It has no oomph to flow anywhere.

Now imagine the opposite. Your river is surrounded on all sides by cement. Nothing gets in. The life that is around cannot be fortified by your waters. Without this kind of communion, your river is devoid of life. It flows with urgency and direction but is not informed by the richness of relationship.

What fuels our internal river is that inner heart pull toward expansion. Along the way, we both are fed and feed others through relationship. This intelligence comes with us everywhere we go. Perhaps if we understood making boundaries as a way to tend to our river, we'd engage with them in a different way.

What Is Running in You?

Take a moment to connect with your own river. Don't worry if you can't feel it in your body. For now, simply imagine it. Does it have smooth stones on the bottom, or is it sandy and tangled with grasses? Is the water brisk, like a high-mountain stream, or warm and playful? What kind of life does your river support? Are there salmon and trout? Alligators?

Now ask, how does my river flow? How are your banks? What do you *tend toward* when making boundaries? This isn't to say you do this *all* the time, but when relationships get hard, what is usually happening?

If your river doesn't have banks, boundaries feel punitive. You're worried about hurting others' feelings. Being there for the people you care about is important to you, even if that means you don't have time for yourself. You may have a parent or caregivers who overextend themselves for others. It may be expected that you behave similarly. You'd like to have more energy to pursue what matters to you, but you're too tired. There's never enough time to do all that's on your plate. You have no problem making friends, but these relationships aren't always satisfying. You're driven by a sense of obligation.

If you're more familiar with cement walls, you may be using boundaries as a way to suppress or control your feelings. They're a way to protect yourself. Your walls impact how you see the world. They are static and come with you into every relationship. Your walls are not based on real-time information. They protect you from what *has* happened or what *could* happen. You have some friends, but no one really "knows" you. You'd like more connection in your life, but most people can't be trusted. You hold on to the relationships you do have even if they aren't satisfying. Friends are hard to come by.

SOMATIC PRACTICE: Boundaries

You can do this practice standing, seated, or lying down. Read over the practice and then determine how you'd like to position yourself. You can also listen to a guided audio version of this practice at http://www.newhar binger.com/50614.

As Oshun showed us when we visited the Nile, what pulls our river is what our heart longs for. This longing informs our boundaries. It's important to note that boundaries aren't something we're aiming to do perfectly one day. We're always going to be learning. They are opportunities to get to know ourselves better.

First ask, What is it that my heart craves in relationships?

Do I want more depth in my relationships? Do I want to be seen, but I'm not allowing others in?

Do I want meaningful relationships that don't leave me feeling drained? Do I show up for others but leave myself?

To do this practice, begin by imagining that near you is a person who is important to you, someone whom you'd like to practice healthy connection with. In this introductory practice, I recommend not choosing your most challenging relationship. Opt instead for someone who is a 5 or 6 on the scale of difficulty rather than a 10.

In your mind's eye, position this person near you. They can be in front of you, to the side, or wherever else you'd like to imagine them.

If your river is banked by cement walls, try the following practice:

As you imagine your chosen person near you, connect to your body in the present moment.

Take a breath to soften.

Soften your eyes.

Soften your jaw.

Soften your throat.

Soften your chest and torso.

Let your breath cascade over you. Can you let it reassure your body? You can be here. You are safe now.

Radiate out from your center in all directions.

Fill your body with your life force, the full torrent of your river. Imagine it flowing and interweaving with the life that is all around.

There's no place in your body that you can't inhabit. Let it flow into your legs, calves, and forearms. You are completely full.

Let these words in: Relationships should allow me to feel this much of myself.

What is the distance that is needed so I can stay this connected?

If you're most familiar with leaving yourself, try the following practice:

As you imagine your chosen person near you, connect to your body in the present moment.

Notice where is your attention pulled.

Can you physically inhale those places?

Imagine bringing your river down into the container of your body. Where are the banks weak?

Where do you feel the impulse to jump out of yourself?

Bring breath here.

When you feel the impulse to leave, can you come back to your breath?

Let these words in: Distance allows for intimacy. Distance and differentiation allow for authenticity. This is connection.

Boundaries Are Love

What boundaries show us is how to center love in our relationship. Without this foundation, we aren't able to properly feel for the distance that is needed in our connection to others. Experiencing love for who we are helps us discern what is for us and what is not. This may feel like a vast distance to cross. How do we truly love ourselves? Easily, volumes could be written on this important topic.

We start by taking a risk. We risk revealing ourselves (to ourselves) over and over again by connecting with the longings of the heart. When we connect to the heart, we slow down and arrive in the present moment. We ask the question: What does my heart want? To ease into this practice, we can begin in small ways. In the morning, we might ask: What do I *really* want for breakfast? How do I want to enjoy it? We find ourselves sitting in a sunbeam with our morning coffee. Or, at an event, we might ask, Whom do I really want to speak to? We initiate conversation with someone we enjoy. This fills us with a kind of appreciation. We embody what it is to really care for ourselves. Reclaiming the erotic happens through simple acts throughout our days. As we do this, we experience how good it feels to be in union with ourselves. Over time, this satisfaction becomes a requirement. The erotic infuses our days and weeks. It extends into the quality of our relationships and our ability to let go of those who aren't truly enriching us. We feel Oshun at our side always reminding us to tend our river.

PART IV

Relate

How do we find peace within the contradiction of both seeking freedom and living inside of systems that require our compliance for survival? Interdependence invites us to a bigger view. It shows us that something *is* emerging, even if it's not at the pace we would prefer. Change is constant. Freedom can be found in how we relate to that change.

CHAPTER 7

Opening to Joy

Sometimes you've just got to live your damn life and be in your body baby.

—Juju Bae

How can we discern if what we're moving toward is motivated by the wisdom of our longings or if something else is at play? For example, is our quest to heal ourselves always coming from the heart? To be committed to our well-being certainly feels virtuous, but can this focus also hold us back?

One of my clients, let's call her Lauren, came to me after ending a longtime relationship with her therapist. "It just wasn't working anymore," she said. "I'm tired of talking. I want to try something else." Lauren knew a lot about how growing up with a not-fully-present parent had impacted her. Her father wasn't in the picture, and her mother worked several jobs, leaving Lauren to mostly fend for herself at a young age. She wanted more intimacy in her relationships but found it hard to open up. She had many acquaintances but no one who really *knew* her. She felt alone.

Early in our work together, Lauren often had a lot to share about her childhood. I noticed that when I asked her what was happening in her body as she recalled her history, she would offer a quick response and then continue. Sometimes she would simply say, "I don't know," or later, when she realized that response would lead me to ask more questions, she would offer something that might keep me from further questioning, such as, "I feel settled," and without missing a beat continue her story. Lauren exhibited a trait I've seen in many of my clients over the years: both a desire to unwind from a painful history and a total dedication to living in that history. Part of Lauren's identity was shaped by what had happened to her.

She defended my attempts to pierce her narrative by inviting her into the present moment through the awareness of her body. Naturally, the light of the present moment was where the vulnerability and intimacy she sought resided. Lauren was both tired of talking and completely committed to it.

Living in Our History

All the people I work with have a history connected to the violence of colonialism. The impacts of what our ancestors faced show up in our communities, our family systems, and our own bodies. We see how being historically forced to prove our value challenges our present-day sense of worth. We see how systemic violence was transfigured into "toughness" and the havoc it's caused. It's brave to be willing to face these difficult truths. I believe that this kind of turning toward is essential for our personal, collective, and societal healing. Without this kind of taking account, the wily arms of the program will trick us into recreating dynamics that support its aims.

However, as we recollect our history, we must also be willing to bring ourselves to face how this history lives in us *in this moment*. Otherwise, we run the risk of our stories about what has happened to us getting in the way of our healing from them in real time. When I'm working with a client who is having a hard time dropping their story, what I'm really working with is a client who wants to change the past. This desire to change the past stems from an often-accurate assessment that what happened then was harmful. Our needs were not met. We keep going back to these moments because this is when we were "broken." Our dedication to our history is a dedication to finally being "fixed" or a way to justify why we are "unfixable." We run through the narrative over and over, solidifying why "we're a mess." The story becomes static. It's the ball and chain we're doomed to carry forever. When we are living in our history, we make ourselves forever deficient. We become a puzzle with a few pieces always located in the past. We are a continual problematic work in progress.

Myth of Colonization: I Am a Project

We make ourselves into projects because we believe there is something fundamentally wrong with us. We may experience moments of ease and pleasure, but our baseline is the steady drum of brokenness. Constantly "working on ourselves" becomes part of our identity. Regardless of the therapies or techniques we try, we never fully arrive. Full acceptance of ourselves is on hold until we see proof that we are better. Our joy gets put on layaway. It's easy to see how this becomes a loop we cannot escape:

I am broken due to my history → *I'm committed to fixing this thing that is wrong* → *My commitment to fixing what is wrong is driven by what is wounded* → *Until I fix what is wrong, I am broken.*

Often, a determination to "work hard" at our healing is an indication that underneath, we've made ourselves into a project. We "project-ify" ourselves because our adult brain, the part of us that knows how to take care of ourselves, is pushed to the background as our younger self emerges. This younger part of ourselves is doing the best it can to "fix" our situation. We believe that the hard work we are doing to heal makes us a "good person." Our ancestors persevered so we could have a better life. Fixing ourselves is the responsible thing to do. This isn't just about us; this is also about our children and their children. There's a lot on the line. How easy it is to justify our status as a project.

When We're Driven by Our Wound

How are we to know if what is driving us is our heart or our wound? Our woundedness acts from a place of self-aggression. It is inherently disembodied. It's running on an old story in our mind that's long outdated. Lauren knew that a connection to her body could be helpful; that's what brought her to work with me. But when it came to actually engaging with her body, she was put off. It was as if her younger self was challenging her, "What is that going to do?" The idea was far more compelling than the actual practice. In addition to coaching, she had tried several other modalities but never stuck with them. When I asked why, she said, "because they didn't work." When I asked how she would know if what she was doing was working, she said she would be happier. However, while a desire to be happy is not unrealistic, happy is not a place that most of us live.

Committed to a story that she was unfixable, Lauren had made the tall order of happiness the required proof that transformation was happening. Here's another example. A client, we'll call her Elise, was picked on in preschool. She was the only Black girl in her class, which is why she believed the other girls wouldn't play with her at recess. This was very painful for Elise, who is naturally social and outgoing. She would bribe the girls to play with her by bringing extra Fruit Roll-Ups to school. When she didn't have extra treats to share, she was distraught. Who would play with her now?

This pattern continued to show up in her adult life. When entering a new group, she tried to "earn" acceptance by offering a compliment, being agreeable, or giving others something tangible they would like. It would be easy to interpret her actions as heartfelt, but knowing more of her story, we see she was acting from her pain. Anytime Elise was welcomed for simply being who she is, she was distrustful. "What was wrong with these people?" She shut down relationships with people who didn't ask something of her. When these more demanding relationships unraveled, she blamed herself for not having better boundaries.

Here are some indications that a desire to heal is actually a form of self-aggression. As you read over this list, ask yourself, do any of these resonate for you? If so, how do you see this playing out in your life?

- You hold an internal mantra that you can never achieve, like, "be better," "be happy," "be good."

- You believe that if you were really committed, you would be better by now.

- You blame yourself completely for your perceived deficiencies.

- You judge yourself and double down on new measures when old wounds resurface.

- You hop from one therapeutic approach to the next, always looking for the thing that's going to "work."

- What else?

SOMATIC PAUSE: Feeling

Take a deep breath. What are you noticing? What thoughts are here? What are you sensing in your body?

Making Friends with the Body

Here's the thing about our bodies. We can poke and prod. We can stomp our feet and make our demands, but the body is going to do what it wants to do. It's going to do what it has learned to do to survive. The body doesn't have any interest in unlearning patterns that have kept it safe. Why would that be a good idea? So, when our wise minds recognize that we're engaging in a pattern that is not helpful and then "gets to work" to fix it, the body usually isn't on board. Say, for example, you grew up in a violent household. Now, you're noticing that anytime there's a hint of disagreement in your relationships, you check out. You see that this isn't helpful, so you work on it. You say, "Okay, I see that I do this. I see why I do this; I'm not going to do it anymore." Well, though the mind has made some plans for your future self, the body hasn't. The pattern continues to arise, and you become more and more frustrated. It's easy to see how one might turn their body and thus themselves into a project. "There's something wrong with me. I need to be less defensive."

When the body feels "project-ified," it reasserts its protective habits even more diligently. It locks down on what has worked to protect itself from not just the external threat but the internal adversary you've now become. Trust collapses in this environment. Everyone's heels are dug in. There must be another way.

Kindness is a bridge into another type of relationship with our body. Connecting with our bodies from a place of kindness builds a sense of trust. We're saying to our bodies, "Hey, I see you. I hear you, and I'm not making you wrong. We can be friends." When we're at ease, we've moved out of a state of fight, flight, freeze, and appease and into a state of availability. We can literally imagine this in our muscles. When our sympathetic nervous system is activated (the one responsible for fight or flight), our muscles are contracted. We're on alert. We're ready to spring into action. When we're at ease, our parasympathetic nervous system is activated. This is the part of our nervous system that signals to the body that we can rest. It is impossible to access the wisdom our muscles hold when we are in an activated state. The deep healing work that many of us long for, the healing of our own stories and those carried in our muscles from our ancestors, requires that we are in a place of ease to access them.

It is only through kindness, through those moments when we drop the project and allow ourselves to trust our inherent nature, that we're able to unwind from the patterns that seek to be unwound in us. There is no rolling up our sleeves and getting to the tough places; there is just reconnecting with the knowing of the heart through the wonder of our senses and our interoception (Remember that word from chapter 3, our multilayered inner knowing?) in each moment.

Kindness: The Crack in the Narrative

When we see how we are being aggressive with ourselves, our awareness opens up possibilities for real healing. This healing begins by meeting ourselves with kindness. Not just any kindness, but tangible, embodied care. In my own life, there are two individuals who have been my greatest teachers in building this kind of relationship with myself. First, let me tell you about my friend Nikki.

Nikki and I met at a meditation retreat and instantly bonded. I knew we would be lifelong friends when she unexpectedly asked me to do the Running Man with her after hours of meditating in silence. Yes, that was exactly what my body wanted to do.

One Saturday, I remember giving her a call. I was feeling quite pleased with myself. I had worked out, I had gone to the grocery store, I had read my dharma books, I had cleaned the house. I had done all the things a "good girl" is supposed to do. And now, with all the doing done, I could rest and drop in with my friend. I asked her how she was. "I'm feeling a little tender," she said calmly, "You know, I just really didn't feel like putting on clothes today. So, I'm wearing my pajamas. And I didn't really want to go outside, so I'm still in bed. And I've been watching this incredible series on Netflix. Then I got hungry, and I ordered myself a pizza. So, I'm eating pizza in my bed."

This was not a confession. There was zero note of anxiety or depression when she shared her day with me. When I asked why she was feeling tender, she said she didn't know. I believed her. Her tone was smooth, loving, and compassionate, like she had wrapped herself in the softest of blankets. I remember being astounded by her lack of apology. How was it possible to be so completely at ease with oneself after a day spent (in my mind) doing nothing? I certainly had days when I couldn't bring myself to complete my "best self" checklist, but I wouldn't share this with anyone. I wouldn't answer the phone. I would be in hiding. If I allowed my body a moment of ease, in the background, shame was always questioning, "Am I going to get stuck there? How far am I setting myself back? I must get back to my routines tomorrow!" What would it mean to be oriented by this sort of kindness? What I saw in Nikki that day I had seen before; I just hadn't recognized it as an asset.

My mother's mother, Grandma Jan, or GJ for short, had a habit of speaking about her body in the third person. She'd say things like, "I'd really like to go, but my body is saying no." Or, "My body doesn't like that."

In her presence, it was 100 percent acceptable to speak to the needs of one's body in any moment, as in, "My body needs a nap," or "My body needs a little treat." To be fair, I took advantage of this as a kid. I'd say things like, "I'd like to eat these peas, but my body is saying no." But even if she suspected I was scapegoating my body, she never questioned it. The body *always* had the final say.

Growing up, the way GJ spoke about her body was kind of an inside family joke. "Oh, what do GJ and her body have to say today?" We held their relationship as an attention-seeking quirk. Why did her body have so many *needs?*

Seeing my wise friend Nikki model embodied kindness, I could now also see what a profound teacher my grandmother had been for so many years. What she was trying to show me is that our bodies deserve to be part of the conversation, that when we make room for how they speak to us, we are making room for our wholeness. She was trying to show me that healing is not about *becoming* something, but about *allowing* who we already are to emerge. Perhaps most importantly though, GJ was trying to show me that regardless of the challenges we face, connecting to the body means opening to joy and, in that, connecting to life.

GJ suffered from chronic illness that for many years made her nauseated and lethargic. She had a troubled childhood and traumatic young adulthood that she didn't speak of. She also had an exquisite relationship to pleasure. Her garden overflowed with the audacious and the exotic. She subscribed to a gourmet chocolate club that delivered monthly boxes of treats. She loved to play card games and board games and really anything we could make into a game. To have a body, even one that was failing, meant to continually open to delight. Her insistence on joy, even amid the difficult, was an insistence on her wholeness. She was not in need of fixing—she had arrived: complex, sometimes grumpy, but unwaveringly in partnership with the full kaleidoscope of her humanity.

Decolonizing Truth: I Am Designed for Joy

I'm not talking about joy in the sense of rainbows and kitten kisses. These moments are nice, but it is an unrealistic expectation to believe that we will always be ebullient. The joy I'm talking about here is the joy of what it means to be in a body—to be alive. Our joy reminds us that there's nowhere we have to go and nothing we have to do to be "better." We are complete. Our joy can hold our many moods, our sorrows, and our grief. It is available to us when old wounds surface, and it can help us inspect and engage in patterns that honor its truth. This kind of joy is accommodating, patient, and kind.

Our bodies are made for joy. Let's take a moment to think about the dynamism of the body. We have skin that can feel the heat of a hot summer sidewalk and the cool of the can of soda we pull from the fridge. We have noses that can recognize the night-blooming jasmine that heralds summer waning into autumn. We have eyes that know light and shadow, shape and color; tongues that taste and crave; and ears that listen and recognize.

Our senses are the tentacles that open us up to our world. There is an inherent gratification in isolating and simply being with whatever is arising in each of these domains. Even if we don't have access to all our senses, our body learns to adapt and still bring us the information from our world through creative means.

We then interpret this information through sensation—through aches and groans, hearts beating, and stomachs dropping. There is an aliveness here that is often what we are seeking when we imagine what it would be like to be "healed." We imagine we'll be more available. We imagine we'll be more authentic. We imagine we'll be more creative. We imagine we'll be more vulnerable. And yet, all of that lives right here, breath by breath. Connecting to the joy of what it means to have a body is the domain of our healing. When we do so, we shift the purpose of our life from "healing" to "living." As controversial as that statement may be, I don't believe that fixing ourselves is the primary project anyone should be committed to.

SOMATIC PRACTICE: Sensorial Arrival

Let's arrive in this moment through the senses together. I'll go first.

In this moment, heavy machinery rattles and clanks as it grades the street outside our home; my dog, Sheena, trots to the kitchen and takes luxuriously sloppy sips from her water bowl; my keyboard clicks. I smell the peanut butter that swan-dived from this morning's apple slice onto my sweatshirt. It's a foggy morning, the shadows are soft, the air is sultry, and the memory of breakfast still lives on my tongue. I am inspired.

Your turn.

Take a moment to tune in to each one of your senses. What are you noticing?

What sensations are present in your body? What does this communicate to you?

This is not to say that everything our bodies perceive is beauty or that we will not be touched by experiences that hurt or pain us. But if we imagine our sense perceptions as permeable tentacles that extend from us and into our greater surroundings, our bodies connect us with the full display of experience. Even amid the difficult and painful, we also find the sacred. It is through our senses that we make *sense* of the phenomenal world. As GJ and Nikki showed me, the body is a gift. We can pull ever closer to us what thrums and buzzes and moves and hums and feel in return its welcome. We can meet ourselves in our aliveness.

SOMATIC PRACTICE: Everyday Richness

Joy lives in the mundane. When we get close enough to any experience, we find it in the details. I'm reminded of a quote from ornithologist Drew Lanham (2022): "I've had those days where nothing is going right, and it seems like there is more coming that's going to go wrong. But in that moment of that little brown bird, that's always so inquisitive, that sings reliably, in that moment, I'm thinking about that wren, I'm not thinking about anything else. That's joy." Lanham points to something essential about our joy. It cannot be taken from us. It is something we can access anytime. It's something we can tuck away and store up for ourselves. It does not answer to anyone. Our joy stands up to acts of harm, degradation, and inequity in a nonviolent way. It communicates our values while at the same time restoring rather than depleting us.

A life that centers joy invites us to be present with our world. We see things not for what we have named them but as our senses perceive them interwoven with life. The following is a practice that can connect us to the richness that is present in our everyday lives.

This exercise has two parts. The first part will require a little planning and perhaps some drive time. The second part can be done at home when you won't be disturbed. You can also listen to a guided audio version of this practice at http://www.newharbinger.com/50614.

Part 1. Take yourself somewhere beautiful. It could be a garden or museum. Give yourself a good amount of time for this exercise, thirty minutes to an hour. Walk the space and make a commitment to let your body guide you. Let yourself be pulled toward something you're curious about or drawn to. It could be a part of the exhibit or garden but doesn't have to be. It could be the railing on the stairway or an unassuming flowering clover.

Get close to this thing. Let yourself get so close to it that you can see its parts.

Be with this thing for ten minutes.

Look at it, touch it (if you can), smell it.

Take it in.

What do you see?

Notice what is happening in your body in being close with it.

Reflect on what you were able to experience through your senses that was not initially present with the naked eye.

Part 2. When you are complete at this destination, take yourself back home and walk your space as you did the location of beauty you just visited. Watch the temptation to judge or plan to "fix." Be with your home environment as if you are in a sacred space.

Walk from room to room, and as you did before, let your body be drawn to an object.

Take it in for ten minutes.

What is it like to see your home in this way?

What joys are waiting for you?

What does this evoke in your body?

Joy and Healing

Our joy isn't some fantastical experience that we ascend to; it is available with our full presence. In a society that's prescribed so many avenues for "project-ifying" ourselves, our joy is regarded as the "reward" for our dedication to healing. But our connection to our joy isn't a reward; it is the healing itself.

When we hold ourselves as a project, we're out of relationship with kindness and joy. We forget that we are whole as we are, intelligent as we are, creative as we are. Our bodies are just waiting for us to partner with them. They want to deliver us to our fullest expression of ourselves, if we can just get out of our own way and land right where we are.

Through our work, Lauren was able to slowly build a relationship with her body in the present moment. She began to see that she avoided residing there because there were often sensations present that she didn't know what to do with. Unfamiliar with tolerating the sensations of vulnerability, she shut down these bodily experiences by retreating to the safety of the familiar. Rather than relating to this as a problem to be fixed, she was able to see it as a wise tactic she had learned early on to take care of her fundamental needs for connection. Because the kind of intimacy she needed was not available to her as a child, she rearranged herself to make it no longer a necessary requirement for love. Our work then was not so much about fixing what she was doing but building her tolerance to be with the aliveness that was already present in her body. Her body knew how to be vulnerable. That capacity wasn't missing. It was her relationship to that capacity that needed an update.

Healing isn't about no longer experiencing discomfort. It isn't about being happy and available all the time. Sometimes we need to close ourselves off. Sometimes we need a day in bed eating pizza and watching Netflix for no reason our minds can justify. Sometimes we need to cry about the chronic pain we're sick and tired of experiencing. It's not what has *happened* to us that governs our ability to heal; it's what we do in the present moment with what *is happening.*

Our bodies bring us to the healing we're ready for. It is there that we find kindness. It is there that we find surrender, intimacy, and strength. It's all right there—a giant wave of vitality just waiting to remind us of our fullness. We hold on to our story because we know it. Like a stone in our pocket, we've rolled it around over and over again. What would it mean to let it go? And, because there is no task to be done and no piece of us that is missing, we are still whole even when we are grasping at what feels safe. Our completeness is never in question, simply our ability to see it.

CHAPTER 8

Cultivating Community

Without community there is no liberation, only the most vulnerable and temporary armistice between an individual and her oppression.

—Audre Lorde

The possibility of joy brings us closer to our world. Over time this invitation can help us see things not just for what they appear to be but also for the intricacies of interrelationship that they represent. Buddhist monk Thich Nhat Hanh was known for encouraging students to see things in this way, "the miracle in the mundane." He might, for example, hold up an orange and ask those before him what they saw. Yes, it is an orange, but what else? Can you see the tree with its roots extended down into the soil? The rains that came and soaked its green leaves? Can you see how the sun came from behind the cloud and touched the moist earth? The buds that became blossoms and the bees that collected their pollen? Can you see the tiny green fruit that warmed to yellow and orange? Watch the hands that plucked and carried it, the hands that stored and drove it, the hands that unpacked and placed it. Now, see it in my hand, this miracle, before I peel and bite.

When we think contemplatively about these interrelationships, we can't deny them. We can imagine the beings who rose before the sun to harvest the berries that now float on our morning yogurt. We can see the oak, wide and dignified, in the old hardwood floors that now creak below our feet. There is beauty and heartbreak in these truths. They bring us to examine where we stand in the nature of things. We see those whom we are dependent on and those who depend on us. Our loss looks back at us in lockstep with our privilege.

How might our world look if more of us saw it through the eyes of interdependence? Would the global community be more committed to addressing climate change? Would poverty, income inequality, and food insecurity even exist? It's not hard to imagine Thich Nhat Hanh, who himself was a dedicated peace activist, holding similar questions as he invited his students to relate to experience through this lens.

The mirage of the program is vested in us not entertaining such inquiries. It distracts us from examining interrelationship with the illusion of a more palatable world. In this world, like the volume knob on a radio, our privilege and loss are turned way down. There's no need to contend with these discomforts. For the right price, any pains we're feeling are easily taken care of. Everything is available and nothing is exhaustible. We can have the life we "dream" of. In some ways, it's more comfortable to live in this world. It numbs us from feeling the continual cycle of life arising and dying before our eyes. We can avoid contending with the grief and hopelessness that many of us don't know what to do with. Instead, we're encouraged to keep hustling for a better tomorrow.

The world of the program is static. It's structured by rules and hierarchies and the myth that if you do it all right, then you'll be free. Recognizing interrelationship counters this view. It instead puts us in contact with a fundamental Buddhist truth. Our life, our world, and all that we hold dear are unstable. Everything is impermanent. From the mountain ranges that stitch together our continents to the cells in our physical bodies, nothing is solid or lasting. Everything is in a state of constant change. As Buddhist teacher Chögyam Trungpa Rinpoche is often quoted, "The bad news is you are falling through the air, nothing to hang on to, no parachute. The good news is, there is no ground." This experience is mightily uncomfortable for a self conditioned to believe that there *is* something to hang on to. The program tells us that if we hang on tightly enough, we'll one day be placed gently on the solid ground of abundance, success, and happiness. The myths we've been deconstructing on this journey are the illusory parachutes we're clutching.

By chapter, they are the parachutes of:

1. I can find work that will prove my value.

2. If I work hard enough, I'll one day earn peace and ease.

3. My body must function correctly to get me where I want to go.

4. The discomfort I feel can be fixed.

5. If I'm the right version of myself, I'll find belonging.

6. My grit is my strength.

7. I'm an imperfect work in progress. I can be better.

All of these point to the undergirding confusions that shape the colonized self.

Our Final Myth of Colonization: I Am Independent

If I am independent, I am in control. I have complete power to address the challenges that plague me. My success depends on me alone. You'll notice that all the parachutes put the self at the center. Everything begins and ends with "me." I can do life on my own. I blame myself for the lack of ease I'm experiencing. And, if I'm struggling, I just need to be better, to work harder. It's not difficult to hear the voice of the program underneath this narrative. If my success is dependent on me alone, so too is my failure. My inability to thrive is divorced from the systems that structure the society I live in. Though they are not designed for my thriving, I believe *I* can win at capitalism. *I* can win at white dominance. *I* can win at the patriarchy. *I* can be the exceptional one. I'll flourish where others have fumbled. It's not that we consciously hold these beliefs, it's that they subconsciously dictate our actions, and that is why they are so poisonous. They are the invisible parachutes we keep reaching for to save ourselves.

This last myth is particularly tricky because, in part, it is true. We are independent. We do have agency. We can make things happen for ourselves. But it is equally true that we are fundamentally interdependent. We reside inside both of these realities. It is because the idea of an independent self is so centralized in Western culture that we must especially lean in to remembering and embodying our interdependence. How did we get so disconnected from this knowing?

Shaped to Be Independent

Societally, we're shown that our self-reliance is an attribute. We're praised for "getting the job done" and "pulling ourselves up by our bootstraps." Even if we don't consciously sign on to these beliefs, we spend time in environments where they are affirmed. From the competitive nature of the academic setting to our workplaces, we're continually encouraged to relate to success as an individual pursuit. In some settings, we're pressured to troubleshoot challenges on our own and avoid taking them to higher-ups unless it is *absolutely necessary*. Needing advice or support from others positions us as less than. We worry that showing that we don't know something will prove that we don't belong.

Culturally, we continually hear stories from "successful" people who claim they achieved what they did solely through their own hard work and dedication. I felt my blood boil when during a 2022 interview, reality TV star Kim Kardashian, who parlayed her social clout into a successful shapewear line, offered the following suggestion: "I have the best advice for women in business. Get your fucking ass up and work. It seems like nobody wants to work these days" (Variety 2022).

I'd like to ask Kim, Who are these women who don't want to work? Everywhere I look, that couldn't be further from the truth. Furthermore, does she attribute her billionaire status to her hard work alone? Where's her acknowledgment of her privilege and the many hands that brought her to where she is?

For many of us, the homes we grew up in are the first places we learned the value of being independent. Perhaps not relying on our caregivers made us the "strong" one. If there was instability in the family, we may have taken on an outsized amount of responsibility at a young age. Maybe at the time, we were proud that we could help, that our family could count on us. Later in life, we learned that being self-sufficient and of service to others could gain us love and acceptance. In our interpersonal relationships, we became the problem-solving friend and partner—the one everyone could go to for help. Rarely though did we ask this of others.

SOMATIC PAUSE: Feeling

Take a deep breath. What are you noticing? What is your relationship to being "strong and independent"? What sensations are present in your body?

Distinct Views of Freedom

We can understand the simultaneity of independence and interconnection by thinking about our own bodies. Our bodies are made of individual cells that are themselves complete. They contain a nucleus, mitochondria, ribosomes, and many other parts that support their functioning. Groupings of cells work in concert to form our heart, lungs, brain, and so forth. How do these cells know what to do? This continues to be discovered. What we do know is that they work in harmony to bring form and function to our physicality. Our individual cells need the body just as much as the body needs our individual cells. Without each other, they cease to exist. If we zoom out, we can imagine such is also true for what we consider the independent self. We are like the individual cells in a body. We are singular and fundamentally interwoven in a larger group body. How we work together determines the health of not only our societies but the planet itself.

Many indigenous communities see this. The truth of interdependence is so primary that when colonizers first arrived in the Americas, the native population was aghast by the foreigners' dismissal of it. Instead of recognizing individual health as intrinsically connected to the health of the whole, European societies equated individualism with a concept of freedom rooted in material gain for a select few. White males were free (within reason) to do whatever is necessary to amass wealth and personal property.

There are accounts as early as the seventeenth century of Native American observers voicing criticism of the colonial way of life. One such voice was that of Kandiaronk, a Huron–Wendat statesman, politician, and highly skilled orator. In *The Dawn of Everything: A New History of Humanity*, authors David Graeber and David Wengrow share excerpts of Kandiaronk's views, as recorded and later published by a French soldier who dialogued with the Wendat chief during his time stationed in Canada. Louis-Armand de Lom d'Arce, Baron de la Hontan, or Lahontan as he was known, became fluent in Algonquian and Wendat and, because he was skeptical of Christianity, claimed native people were more willing to speak frankly with him about their own views. In the late seventeenth century, Kandiaronk shared with him the pitfalls of a money-centric society.

> *I have spent six years reflecting on the state of European society, and I still can't think of a single way they act that's not inhumane, and genuinely think this can only be the case, as long as you stick to your distinctions of "mine" and "thine." I affirm that what you call money is the devil of devils; the tyrant of the French, the source of all evils; the bane of souls and slaughterhouse of the living. To imagine one can live in the country of money and preserve one's soul is like imagining one could preserve one's life at the bottom of a lake* (Graeber and Wengrow 2021, 54).

For Kandiaronk, money-ruled societies invariably were afflicted by personal self-interest over any possibility of actual freedom. The indigenous way of life considered freedom a result of living interdependently among a community. If anyone's basic needs were not met, for example, not having enough food to eat or a place to shelter from the elements, freedom would not be possible. Instead, that person would be imprisoned by the continual fight to do what was necessary to survive. If one member of the community was not free, no one was.

Father Pierre Biard, who in 1608 was assigned to evangelize the Mi'kmaq in Nova Scotia, journaled about his frustration with this Native American societal view.

> *They consider themselves better than the French: "for," they say, "you are always fighting and quarreling among yourselves; we live peaceably. You are envious and are all the time slandering each other; you are thieves and deceivers; you are covetous, and are neither generous nor kind; as for us, if we have a morsel of bread, we share it with our neighbor"* (Graeber and Wengrow 2021, 38).

What most irritated Biard was that the Mi'kmaq considered themselves "richer" than the French. Though the French had more material possessions, "they had other, greater assets: ease, comfort, and time" (Graeber and Wengrow 2021, 38). In other words, the Mi'kmaq were free.

The importance of prioritizing the well-being of the individual within the care of the collective is a feature of indigenous communities across the globe. Elder Malidoma Somé, whom we met in chapter 2, shares how among the Dagara of Burkina Faso, the collective is responsible for strengthening the individual and recognizing collectively what cannot be accomplished alone. He writes:

> *This acknowledgment is also an objection against the isolation of individuals and individualism by a society in service of the Machine. What we want is to create community that meets the intrinsic need of every individual* (Somé 1993, 49).

This is not to romanticize or gloss over the fact the violence occurred in indigenous communities as well. However, the scale between what occurred within native populations and the genocide enacted by Western countries is wholly different. Perhaps some of this difference is rooted in differing experiences and views of community. The indigenous way of life, the way of life from which we stem, realizes freedom as the result of moving as a unified whole to secure resources for all in the community. This is distinctly divergent from the European view, which holds freedom as both the result of and a necessary requirement for securing personal material gain.

SOMATIC PAUSE: Aligning Body and Mind

What is freedom in your body? Take a moment to imagine yourself at your most free. This could be from an experience in your history or how you might imagine it could be. What are you doing? Who are you with?

Holding this image of yourself, feel into the relationships, past and present, supporting you. Can you see yourself in the same way that Thich Nhat Hanh invited his students to see the orange? What necessary interconnections are required for this experience of freedom?

Notice what thoughts arise alongside the sensations present in your body.

Our Final Decolonizing Truth: I Am Interdependent

We are interdependent. We are enfolded in all of life. All of history is enfolded in us. We can feel for and relate to our dependency on one another, but we cannot control it. We need each other to pave our roads, to grow our food, to sew our clothes, to teach our children, and to heal us from our ailments. Our ability to tolerate uncertainty is directly tied to our ability to recognize interdependence.

When our plans don't go as we hoped, when we're unexpectedly impacted by loss, when we're overcome with feelings of love or grief, there is an opening in our "agenda as usual." Our recognition of interdependence, that a larger fabric of connection is holding us, helps us navigate the unknown without leaving our bodies and spinning into anxiety. We are relieved from "figuring it all out" and instead brought to trust our present experience. In my own life, one of the richest places to flex into this kind of knowing is through group process work.

Meeting the Group Body

As a facilitator, I hold my role as that of a listener to "the group body." The group body is who we are as a collective. I'm feeling for how we want to move together, the wisdom that is ready to surface, the irruptions primed to open more space, the solutions arising to questions yet formed. I hold the collective as sacred. It is a living, breathing, moving, sensing body that in and of itself naturally moves toward its thriving. As one might imagine, this journey waxes and wanes with varying degrees of comfort. It's difficult to bump up against others' requests, boundaries, and conflicting perspectives. In these moments, I'm eager to retreat to the comfort of being an individual self. It all just feels so exhausting. But, if I can take off the hat of requiring my agenda, more relaxation is possible. There is a smoothing aspect within this choreography. Like rocks in a rock tumbler, our edges are softened by feeling each other's presence.

Building our capacity to be in the microcosm of a group body can strengthen our trust in the macrocosmic truth of our interdependence. Even when things are not going as we want, when we're vehemently opposed to a situation or fully overwhelmed, we can allow our anger or passion to be held by this larger container. To be embodied in a world fraught with inequity and suffering requires sensing our interdependence. It is the only sustainable way. Otherwise, the difficulties we confront will burn us up. We turn ourselves into superhumans believing the fate of the planet rests squarely on our shoulders alone. When we're not impassioned, it's easy to see the flaws in believing we alone can solve climate change or racial injustice or, conversely, that there's nothing that our small bodies can do. In the heat of battle, we can find ourselves worked up and our nervous systems dysregulated as we take on more than we can hold. The truth of interdependence shows us another way. Yes, we are individual bodies, but we are also interwoven in a fabric of connection. We can let that support hold and settle us. How do we begin to feel for this reality? Not just conceptually but in our bodies? We find our place within the smaller group body. We recognize our place in community.

An Alternative View of Community

We do not live in the intact communities of our indigenous ancestors. We presuppose that until we have these kinds of connections, we will never find ease. We long for community while at the same time, well-versed at being independent selves, we are a little scared of it. We want to be seen, but only so much. We hunger to let others in, but only so far. I believe all of this is understandable and workable. Though our world looks much different than that of our ancestors, we can have a satisfying experience of being supported by a collective. But before we explore how we "do" community, let's first look at what I mean by community.

Community emerges from a shared recognition of interdependence. It is not necessarily the people who live near us or those who we see frequently at this or that social gathering. Nor is it the folks who share our interests, as in, the foodie community, the yoga community, the writing community, and so forth. It's not uncommon that those who lack these kinds of connections believe they don't have community. However, the people we see (or don't see) frequently aren't our community. Even those we choose to kick it with regularly aren't necessarily community. I would simply call these gatherings of people. A shared recognition of interdependence can emerge from a gathering but is not in and of itself a community.

If we follow the example of the Mi'kmaq, a community understands its well-being as being *tied* together. As such, it evokes a sense of real care. These are the beings (notice I didn't just say people) we are held by. This understanding of community puts us in contact with the indigenous understanding of freedom.

It's not uncommon in the West to see quasi-communities. From coworking spaces to personal development workshops, it's very popular right now to tout the goal of "building a sense of community." In a quasi-community, the word "community" is used repeatedly, but it doesn't *feel* like a community. Everyone is "nice," but we don't know these people. Furthermore, they don't know us. In a quasi-community, we may believe that if we just tried harder to "be a part of the community," we'd have the kind of connections we long for. Maybe others really do feel a sense of community. Is it just us? When we are asking these questions, we are in red-flag territory. I would instead invite deeper inquiry that doesn't centralize oneself as the problem. We might first ask, What is going on with the money? Is someone getting paid by our presence and selling us "community," or are *we* getting paid to be there? I'm not saying this is bad or wrong. But this is not a recipe for true community. When we go into these spaces seeking it, we're often disappointed (and internalize the experience as meaning something faulty about ourselves).

The second question I would ask is, What is our collective relationship to time? Are we upholding a set agenda, or are we moving with the needs and arisings of the group? Are our interactions bound by time? Will I see these people in my normal life or only when we're scheduled to be together? Again, this isn't a judgment of time-bound interactions. In many ways, agreeing to an agenda makes relating feel safe and possible among large groups of unknown bodies. However, being in each other's lives only when we are scheduled to be so is not community.

Money and time are the reality of capitalism. These factors are primary (and often unconsciously so) in all our gathering spaces unless consciously attended to. When money and time conflict with the needs of community, they will invariably come first. This doesn't mean we won't be kind to each other or try to help each other, but our extension of ourselves has a limit. We take on supporting others in our community as personal good deeds rather than a natural function of the collective we are in. What happens, for example, when participation in the community is contingent on payments, such as membership fees, classes, or dues? If we're not able to pay, perhaps there are sliding-scale or work-trade options, but often these are not continually sustainable. We aren't able to continually trade our time for tuition because we need to make money to support ourselves. The sliding-scale option is still not feasible or is offered to only certain participants. We may feel guilty for asking for these supports in an ongoing way. When faced with these challenges, we fear we are at risk of losing the community we've invested in.

As Kandiaronk emphasized, centralizing money disconnects us from experiences of community. Rather than a community, what we are in is an exchange of goods and services. We can exchange many things—training, skills, counseling, therapy—and feel satisfied in these transactions. We can't, however, exchange community. We can't exchange belonging. A community puts its members' needs first. Enough trust has been built that our ability to do so does not compromise our individual basic needs. For example, I can give my time to be with someone who is grieving, and I know I will still have dinner for my children because someone will share their food with me. This explains why after a gathering, it's so hard to stay in touch with the "community" that was created there. It wasn't a community. It was a gathering of bodies with similar interests.

I think it's important to take pressure off ourselves from believing that in every space we enter, we should find community. Most often, that is not the case. Very often spaces that are designed for learning, sharing, and growing together are not designed for community. They can birth community, but they are not built primarily for it. To be in community requires that I care for your needs alongside my own. Our care for each other is a foundational shared value. We can still lead with our values when in these kinds of spaces. From our places of employment to shared interest groups, our interest in and kindness toward each other is what often distinguishes pleasurable interactions from those we dread. When this is present, we feel a sense of kinship with others. However, this in and of itself won't satisfy our human needs to be truly *held* by each other. Time and again, I've counseled friends who have been disappointed by their community when it didn't show up for them in a time of need. While painful, I must ask, Why do you believe this is your community?

In our own lives, we can evaluate whether we are truly in a community by asking the following questions: Is there conscious attention placed on holding and being there for one another? How is this modeled? Would these people give me money if I needed it? Would I give money to them? Is this normalized? Do we celebrate together? Do we grieve? Because the term "community": is so often used to describe a gathering of bodies with similar interests, the kind of community that answers yes to the above questions is what we could call instead a "beloved community."

Recognizing Beloved Community

How are we to find such compadres to share life with in this intimate way? An orientation toward going out to get something is once again the orientation of the program. We can't buy our way in. We can't put on our shiniest selves at a networking event and get it. Instead, connecting with beloved community means doing the opposite of what we think we should do to build community: we start close to home.

Because we are fundamentally interdependent, every one of us is supported by nutritive relationships. Some of these relationships are far from our conscious seeing of them, but many others are right in front of us. Our understanding of beloved community begins with this recognition. We ask, Who are the beings and what are the landscapes that I'm already intimately shaped by? Then, with intention, we *take care* of these relationships in a way that honors their importance in our life. Taking care means not only making central the well-being of these dynamic others, but also letting them center our well-being in return. Our willingness to open to them and let them support us is a gift for them as well. This is where we practice letting go of being an independent self and stretch into living our interdependence. Programmed to be strong and self-sufficient, it's naturally foreign to many of us to extend ourselvers in this way. I would say it's often not even safe. There is intelligence in the resistance we feel. We can trust the push-pull that exists rather than make it mean there's something wrong with us. It's very possible that we're in a quasi-community where vulnerability isn't actually a good idea. Our body can help us discern what's going on, but to do so we must build that muscle. We titrate our ability to connect with beloved community by opening to what is already close in and trustworthy.

Who are the most important relationships in your life? If you're not comfortable with people, you might ask, Who are the nonpeople you can be yourself with? Our beloved community could include the big tree we pass on our morning walk or the ravens we see hopping and diving toward our driveway on trash day. It could be a pet or even a large natural feature, like the ocean or a favorite trail. As we recognize our dependence on these beings, our world becomes larger. It feels good to decenter ourselves and offer care and attention. It feels incredible to recognize that care and attention coming back to us. To feel known. This watering of our community helps us feel less alone. We feel taken care of. This is the ground that helps our beloved community grow. In time, these connections broaden organically. We may join a collective that's dedicated to protecting the local beach we love. Or maybe we find ourselves wanting to protect the little ones we see walking to school each morning and join a local chapter of Moms Demand Action. Our beloved community expands by meeting others similarly oriented by care. We don't have to push for it or gather these beings like shiny marbles; we let our body recognize them and naturally extend us out.

JOURNAL: Aligning Body and Mind

Give yourself thirty minutes to reflect on the following questions. Don't overthink your answers; let whatever arises arise. Let your answers come forward with more than words. Feel free to draw, doodle, color, move, or do however else your body wants to express itself.

Who are five beings that you'd like to practice beloved community with? I chose five because it feels like a good manageable number, but don't feel pressured to stick to this. Again, these need not be people you're already in deep connection with. What's most important is that you have a *desire* to be. Your community can include humans and nonhumans alike.

Make a list of who your beloved community is right now. Then take some time to think about how you might offer care to them and in what ways you may request their care in return. For example, I will bring water to my favorite redwood. When I'm feeling overwhelmed, I will visit this friend and ask her to help me ground.

I recommend letting these beings know that you'd like to be in this relationship with them. Share your commitment toward care and ask for their insights. If these beings are nonhuman, feel for their responses in your body. This is a powerful way to be in communication. Our opening to this possibility of beloved community in this way helps us see that our needs can be met by more than just our partner or a friend. There is a wealth of nutritive relationship right where we are.

SOMATIC PRACTICE: Feeling for Interdependence

You are already a part of a beloved community. You can open to feel this interdependence in your body. This practice can be done anywhere, though I recommend doing it outside. Give yourself five to ten minutes. You can also listen to a guided audio version of this practice at http://www.newharbinger .com/50614.

Take a moment to determine how your body would like to be: sitting, standing, lying down.

When you arrive, do a centering practice.

Now, bring your awareness particularly to your width.

Extend out from your width; open your periphery to include your environment. Extend your awareness to another being nearby. This could be a pet, plant, or person in a neighboring area. Now, narrow your periphery to release this contact with another. Our width is where we feel our interconnection. Experiment with expanding your width to feel this in all directions. Expand out to:

> Feel the beings below, the intelligence of the worms and crawling bugs.

> Feel the beings above, the birds, the flying insects.

> Feel the beings on your plane, the plants and four-legged animals

> Feel the beings inside, all the tiny organisms that live in your gut. To them you are a universe.

What sensations are present in your body from noticing interrelationships?

It is often said that the next Buddha will be a community. I believe this could be true. I've often reflected, *Gosh I hope I'm still alive; I hope I might be a part of such a community—to experience true liberation.* Sometimes this longing shows up as urgency. Why can't we be together now? Why can't we be free? I must tear down all that is standing in the way. I'm ready for the ease, comfort, and time that the Mi'kmaq spoke of. I'm ready to live by the values of Kandiaronk—to be brought to a richer human experience by abolishing hierarchy and establishing meaning and purpose within a collective.

But this is not the world we live in. How do we find peace within the contradiction of both seeking freedom and living inside of systems that require our compliance for survival? Interdependence invites us to a bigger view. It shows us that something *is* emerging, even if it's not at the pace we would prefer. Alongside that which is difficult there is also a co-arising of that which is life supporting. Because change is constant, we are not stuck in the world we have. We can imagine a more liberated society. We can embody now a world that truly affirms Black and brown bodies and cares for all species and the planet. Though we may not see the realization of these dreams in our lifetime, by living this in our day-to-day through decolonization practices that affirm our values and truly care for ourselves and those we love, we find peace.

Conclusion: Freedom Is Now

While much is needed on a social and political level to be truly free, my aim with this book and these practices is to support Black and brown bodies in recognizing that we don't have to wait until external circumstances recognize our right to liberation. We can practice it now. The Decolonizing Truths we've explored in each chapter support organizing ourselves in this way. Our freedom lives in our slowing down, in our engagement with ritual practices that open us to spiritual intelligence, in our allowing and trusting of bodily sensation, in our understanding of our uniqueness alongside our fundamental similarity, in our taking care of the aliveness that flows through us, and in our opening to the everyday joys that our bodies are designed for. It's all right here. Or, put another way, the more we tune in to our internal radio frequency, the stronger and clearer that channel gets. By listening more completely, we extend our capacity to be in relationship with all that is life supporting and ready to meet us.

In numerology, the number 8 signifies the joining of heaven and earth. Our ending here is by design. Joining heaven and earth means bringing our ideas into practice, into our body, and into our actions. This union is a source of power. It requires building in collaboration with ourselves and those who emerge to create with us. Because you are here, I trust you are one of those people. We are at the end, and in many ways at the beginning. Now we feel. Now we trust. Now we be with each other.

Thank You

I would first like to acknowledge the ancestors. Without your guidance, this book would not have been. Many times, I sat at my altar wondering what was next or how to move forward. Your steady guidance always came. Thank you for the ideas in the middle of the night.

To my partner, Clay Bennett, thank you for your incredible patience, unwavering encouragement, and always to-the-point feedback. I love you.

Mom and Dad, you never doubted my unconventional path and gave me total permission to be me. Thank you for being a safe container to grow, explore, and express.

To all the beings who've I had the pleasure to work with, you are the heart of this book. Your bravery and commitment to these practices inspires me. I hope you see this reflected on the page.

Thank you to my mentors and teachers: Soyinka Rahim, Cynthia Winton-Henry, Phil Porter, Sandy Sargraves, Charlene Leung, Rev. angel Kyodo Williams, Dr. Rae Johnson, Mo Drescher, Wendy Haines, Staci Haines, Richard Strozzi-Heckler, Sandra Ladley, and Stephen Murphy-Shigematsu.

Dina Buck, this book would not be what it is without your insights early on. Thank you for talking me into my wisdom time and time again.

Catherine Hollander, your kindness, encouragement, and understanding of the creative journey was a balm many times. Thank you for letting me lean on you. Thank you for your willingness to support this work—even under a tight deadline.

Members of my chosen family, LeeAnn Stevens, Monu Singh, Nikki Robinson, Lucy Wallace, Katrin Welch, Kristie Wachtor, Annie-Rose London, and Julie Morse, thank you for sitting in a virtual circle with me and championing this possibility from the get-go.

Chetna Mehta, thank you for your invitation to write for *The Moon Times Digest* from Mosaiceye on the topic of Decolonizing the Body, which served as a seed for this book.

To my friends at New Harbinger, thank you Jennye Garibaldi for finding me and encouraging this project and thank you Gretel Hakanson and Madison Davis for your deft eye and brilliant edits.

Dana Newman and Lisa Tener, you held my hand early on.

Finally, thank you, kind reader, for engaging with and sharing this book. Thank you for imagining and practicing liberation with me. May your efforts multiple tenfold.

Resources

The following have shaped many of the perspectives in this book. Please read, share, and enjoy.

The Colonial Project

A People's History of the United States by Howard Zinn. Harper Collins, 1980.

"Is Capitalism Racist?" by Nicholas Lemann, *The New Yorker*, May 25, 2020.

The Dawn of Everything: A New History of Humanity by David Graeber and David Wengrow. Farrar, Strause, and Giroux, 2021.

"The 1619 Project" by Nikole Hannaj-Jones. *The New York Times Magazine.*

Decolonizing

Braiding Sweetgrass: Indigenous Wisdom, Scientific Knowledge, and the Teachings of Plants by Robin Wall Kimmerer. Milkweed Editions, 2015.

Developing Stamina for Decolonizing Higher Education: A Workbook for Non-Indigenous People by Sharon Stein, Cash Ahenakew, Elwood Jimmy, et al., and Higher Education Otherwise

How to Do Nothing: Resisting the Attention Economy by Jenny Odell. Melville House, 2019.

Conversations About the Productivity Paradox, PowerPoint presentation by Move to End Violence. Available at https://movetoendviolence.org/resources/the-productivity-paradox-a-reflection-tool/

Racial/Cultural Identify

Black Skin, White Masks by Frantz Fanon. Grove Press, 2008.

Bone Black: Memories of Girlhood by bell hooks. Henry Holt, 1996.

"Erykah Badu Discovers Her African Ancestry," video. May 20, 2014. https://www.youtube.com/watch?v=YXtUomMjscw&t=2s.

When Half Is Whole: Multiethnic Asian American Identities by Stephen Murphy-Shigematsu. Stanford University Press, 2012.

Body Acceptance

Hearing Our Own Voice podcast hosted by Melissa Toler. https://www.melissatoler.com/podcast

Stop Fighting Food video series hosted by Isabel Foxen Duke. http://stopfightingfood.com/

The Body Is Not an Apology: The Power of Radical Self-Love by Sonya Renee Taylor (book and workbook. Berrett-Koehler Publishers. 2018.

Reclaim Ugly Digest blog by Vanessa Rochelle Lewis. https://reclaimugly.org/

Future Visioning

Finding Our Way podcast hosted by Prentis Hemphill. https://www.findingourwaypodcast.com/

How to Survive the End of the World podcast hosted by the Brown Sisters. https://www.endoftheworldshow.org/

How We Show Up: Reclaiming Family, Friendship, and Community by Mia Songbird. Hachette, 2020.

Undrowned: Black Feminist Lessons from Marine Mammals by Alexis Pauline Gumbs. AK Press, 2020.

Spiritual Practices

A *Little Juju* podcast hosted by Juju Bae. https://www.jujubae.com/podcast

Jambalaya: The Natural Woman's Book of Personal Charms and Practical Rituals by Luisah Teish. HarperCollins 1985.

Ritual: Power, Healing and Community by Malidoma Patrice Somé. Lulu Press, 2020.

Shambhala: The Sacred Path of the Warrior by Chögyam Trungpa. Shambhala, 2007.

Somatics

Already Free: Buddhism Meets Psychotherapy on the Path of Liberation by Bruce Tift. Sounds True, 2015.

Move: What the Body Wants by Cynthia Winton-Henry and Phil Porter. Northstone, 2004

Oppression and the Body: Roots, Resistance, and Resolutions, Christine Caldwell and Lucia Bennett Leighton, eds. North Atlantic Books, 2018.

The Art of Somatic Coaching: Embodying Skillful Action, Wisdom, and Compassion by Richard Strozzi-Heckler. North Atlantic Books, 2014.

The Politics of Trauma: Somatics, Healing, and Social Justice by Staci Haines. North Atlantic Books, 2019.

References

Akómoláfé, B. n.d. "The Times Are Urgent: Let's Slow Down," https://www
.bayoakomolafe.net/post/the-times-are-urgent-lets-slow-down.

Allison, S. N., director. 2021. *Eyes on the Prize: Hallowed Ground.*
Documentary film, HBO Max Originals, https://www.hbomax.com
/feature/urn:hbo:feature:GYQ1PRAGVlcLCJwEAAAA9.

Brown, B. 2021. *Atlas of the Heart: Mapping Meaningful Connection and the
Language of Human Experience.* New York: Random House.

Clance, P. R., and S. A. Imes. 1978. "The Impostor Phenomenon in
High Achieving Women: Dynamics and Therapeutic Intervention."
Psychotherapy: Theory, Research and Practice 15, no. 3 (Fall): 241–247.
https://mpowir.org/wp-content/uploads/2010/02/Download-IP-in-High
-Achieving-Women.pdf.

Demby, G., and S. M. Meraji. 2017. "A Prescription for 'Racial Imposter
Syndrome.'" *Code Switch*, podcast. NPR, June 6, 2017. https://one.npr
.org/?sharedMediaId=528816293:531824445.

EMAVoicesOfTheEarth. 2012. "Earth and Water Reverence; Story of Oshun
Leaving the Earth (Part 5/7)," video. June 29, 2012. https://www.youtube
.com/watch?v=pM5MOS6_SEw.

Fanon, F. 1952. *Black Skin, White Masks.* New York: Grove Press.

Graeber, D., and D. Wengrow. 2021. *The Dawn of Everything: A New History
of Humanity.* New York: Farrar, Straus, and Giroux.

Haines, S. 2019. *The Politics of Trauma: Somatics, Healing, and Social Justice.*
Berkeley: North Atlantic Books.

Hignett, K. 2018. "What Is Impostor Syndrome? Michelle Obama Says She
Suffers from Common Psychological Phenomenon." *Newsweek.* December
4, 2018. https://www.newsweek.com/what-impostor-syndrome-michelle
-obama-says-she-suffers-common-psychological-1242991.

Jones, T., director. 2021. *14 Peaks: Nothing Is Impossible*. Little Monster Films, 1 hr., 35 min. https://www.netflix.com/title/81464765.

Kimmerer, R. W. 2015. *Braiding Sweetgrass: Indigenous Wisdom, Scientific Knowledge, and the Teachings of Plants*. Minneapolis: Milkweed Editions.

Kochhar, R., and A. Cilluffo. 2017. "How Wealth Inequality Has Changed in the US Since the Great Recession, by Race, Ethnicity and Income." Pew Research Center. November 1, 2017. https://www.pewresearch.org/fact-tank/2017/11/01/how-wealth-inequality-has-changed-in-the-u-s-since-the-great-recession-by-race-ethnicity-and-income/.

Lanham, D. 2022 "Pathfinding Through the Improbable." *On Being with Krista Tippett*, podcast. January 28, 2021. https://onbeing.org/programs/drew-lanham-pathfinding-through-the-improbable/.

Lorde, A. 2007. *Sister Outsider: Essays and Speeches*. Berkeley: Crossing Press.

McZeal, A. 2021. "Decolonial Somatic Approaches," PowerPoint presentation. Embodied Social Justice Summit, virtual. April 21, 2021. https://www.embodiedsocialjusticesummit.com/schedule-2021

Odell, J. 2019. *How to Do Nothing: Resisting the Attention Economy*. Brooklyn: Melville House.

Okayplayer, "Erykah Badu Discovers Her African Ancestry," video. May 20, 2014. https://www.youtube.com/watch?v=YXtUomMjscw&t=2s.

Somé, M. P. 1997. *Ritual: Power, Healing, and Community*. New York: Penguin Compass.

Starhawk. 1989. *Truth or Dare: Encounters with Power, Authority, and Mystery*. San Francisco: HarperOne.

Taylor, S. R. 2018. *The Body Is Not an Apology: The Power of Radical Self-Love*. Oakland, CA: Berrett-Koehler Publishers.

Tulshyan, R., and J.-A. Burey. 2021. "End Imposter Syndrome in Your Workplace." *Harvard Business Review*. July 14, 2021. https://hbr.org/2021/07/end-imposter-syndrome-in-your-workplace.

Variety. 2022. "Kim Kardashian's Business Advice: 'Get Your F**king Ass Up and Work,'" video. March 9, 2022. https://www.youtube.com/watch?v=XX2izzshRmI.

Kelsey Blackwell is a cultural somatics practitioner and writer dedicated to supporting women of color to trust and follow the guidance of the body so we may powerfully radiate our worth, dignity, and wisdom in a world which sorely needs this brilliance. As a facilitator, coach, and guest speaker, she has brought abolitionist-embodied practices to such diverse groups as riders on Bay Area Rapid Transit trains to students at Stanford University. She works one-on-one with clients, as well as leads the eight-week group program, Decolonizing the Body. Kelsey is author of the viral article, *Why People of Color Need Spaces Without White People*, published by *The Arrow Journal*. She is certified InterPlay Leader, Strozzi Somatic Coach, and holds a master's degree in publishing from the Medill School of Journalism at Northwestern University. In addition to being impactful, Kelsey believes working toward personal and collective liberation must also bring joy. She lives in San Francisco, CA.

Foreword writer **Christena Cleveland, PhD**, is a social psychologist, public theologian, and activist. She is author of *God Is a Black Woman*, and founder of the Center for Justice + Renewal, which helps justice advocates sharpen their understanding of the social realities that maintain injustice while also stimulating the soul's enormous capacity to resist and transform those realities.

Real change *is* possible

For more than forty-five years, New Harbinger has published proven-effective self-help books and pioneering workbooks to help readers of all ages and backgrounds improve mental health and well-being, and achieve lasting personal growth. In addition, our spirituality books offer profound guidance for deepening awareness and cultivating healing, self-discovery, and fulfillment.

Founded by psychologist Matthew McKay and Patrick Fanning, New Harbinger is proud to be an independent, employee-owned company. Our books reflect our core values of integrity, innovation, commitment, sustainability, compassion, and trust. Written by leaders in the field and recommended by therapists worldwide, New Harbinger books are practical, accessible, and provide real tools for real change.

 **newharbinger**publications

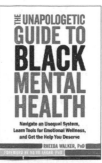

Did you know there are **free tools** you can download for this book?

Free tools are things like **worksheets**, **guided meditation exercises**, and **more** that will help you get the most out of your book.

You can download free tools for this book—whether you bought or borrowed it, in any format, from any source—from the New Harbinger website. All you need is a NewHarbinger.com account. Just use the URL provided in this book to view the free tools that are available for it. Then, click on the "download" button for the free tool you want, and follow the prompts that appear to log in to your NewHarbinger.com account and download the material.

You can also save the free tools for this book to your **Free Tools Library** so you can access them again anytime, just by logging in to your account! Just look for this button on the book's free tools page.

+ Save this to my free tools library

If you need help accessing or downloading free tools, visit **newharbinger.com/faq** or contact us at **customerservice@newharbinger.com**.